*Freud
and
Nabokov*

Geoffrey Green

Freud and Nabokov

University of Nebraska Press
Lincoln and London

Copyright © 1988 by the
University of Nebraska Press
All rights reserved
Manufactured in the United
States of America
The paper in this book meets
the minimum requirements of
American National Standard
for Information Sciences-
Permanence of Paper for
Printed Library
Materials, ANSI Z39.48-1984.
Typeset by Keystone Typesetting Co.,
Orwigsburg, PA
Printed by Edwards Brothers, Inc.,
Ann Arbor, MI
Typeface:
Text: Galliard 9½ on 14 pts.
Display: Galliard 24 pts. ital. b.f.
Futura 9 on 14 pts.
Library of Congress Cataloging
in Publication Data
Green, Geoffrey, 1951–
Freud and Nabokov /
by Geoffrey Green.
p.   cm.
Bibliography: p.
ISBN 0-8032-2130-4 (alk paper)
1. Nabokov, Vladimir Vladimirovich,
1899–1977—Knowledge—Psychology.
2. Freud, Sigmund,
1856–1939—Influence.
3. Psychoanalysis and literature.
I. Title.
PS3527.A15Z724   1988
813'54—dc19   87-16589   CIP

to Marcia

CONTENTS

ACKNOWLEDGMENTS

I would like to thank the following individuals who read the manuscript and contributed valuable suggestions: Jackson Cope, Leslie Fiedler, John Halperin, Marcus Klein, Charles Nicol, and Max Schulz.

I am grateful to Stephen Arkin, Daniel Rancour-Laferriere, Alan Elms, Beverly Lyon Clark, and Phyllis Roth for inviting me to present portions of this work (in modified form) at San Francisco State University, the University of California at Davis, and the annual Vladimir Nabokov Society meetings of 1984 and 1986.

As always, I am glad to have friends and students whose vigorous conversation helped develop my ideas.

It gives me great pleasure to mention here the special contribution of Robert Scholes, my teacher and friend, who read the manuscript in its entirety. It was in his class at Brown University sixteen years ago that I first was inspired to wrestle with Nabokov's *Pale Fire*.

I owe a great deal to the loving encouragement and support of Marvin and Martha Green, my parents.

My wife, Marcia, read each page as it came off the printer and offered insightful suggestions. Her user-friendly enthusiasm and superior knowledge of computers were an invaluable assistance as I wrote for the first time on a word processor. Her time, concern, and energy were unfailing. This book would never have been written without her.

INTRODUCTION

A book on Sigmund Freud and Vladimir Nabokov might appear initially to be the outgrowth of a perverse or mischievous sensibility. There is no reason to believe that Freud ever read Nabokov (or V. Sirin, his nom de plume, for that matter) or that he was aware of Nabokov's existence. To make matters worse, Nabokov hated Freud and psychoanalysis with a passion: he sustained the grandest and most extravagant contempt for psychoanalysis known in modern literature. A work devoted to Freud and Nabokov would seem to be the occasion for a psychoanalysis of Nabokov's characters, or a psychoanalytical discussion of Nabokov's aversion to Freud, or else a principled recounting of the multitudinous criticisms that Nabokov wielded against Freud. But I intend to do none of these things.

Until recently, critics of the psychoanalytical persuasion would refrain, for the most part, from interpreting Nabokov's works. This reticence was sensible and appropriate since Nabokov had all but constructed flashing, luminescent "no trespassing" signs—specifically directed at Freudians—to keep away from his terrain. More meaningful, perhaps, was the recognition that Nabokov's hostility and elaborate warnings and alleged "booby traps" within the novels were all so transparent: such an expansive aversion to psychoanalysis proceeded as much from an intellectual rejection as it did from colossal resistance to the insights psychoanalysis might provide about repressed materials. The implicit idea was that in some sense Nabokov was neurotic to fear Freud so intensively.

Nabokovians, on the other hand, since they tended to follow the master's lead in all things literary, certainly until his death in 1977, did not exempt psychoanalysis from the list of contemptibles. Why did Nabokov detest Freud so much? Obviously, because Freud is so deserving of scorn, etc. All things psychoanalytical were perceived *through* Nabokov, as it were, in much the same way that Pnin is unreliably presented by his antithetical narrator. Thus Freud was conceived as a genuinely demonic figure, an enemy of freedom, a distorter of minds comparable to totalitarian dictators. (An exception would be provided by a few recent critics who have sought to explore Nabokov from a psychoanalytic turn: Alan C. Elms, Leo Schneiderman, and J. P. Shute.)

I find both these "traditional" positions to be wanting. Certainly, Nabokov's phobia could be described as illustrating Freud's 1910 formulation that

> psycho-analysis is seeking to bring to conscious recognition the things in mental life which are repressed; and everyone who forms a judgement on it is himself a human being, who possesses similar repressions and may perhaps be maintaining them with difficulty. They are therefore bound to call up the same resistance in him as in our patients; and that resistance finds it easy to disguise itself as an intellectual rejection. (*Five Lectures on Psycho-Analysis*, 39)

2

But the label of a neurotic aversion serves oddly to diminish what is so fertile and suggestive in Freud's 1908 essay, "Creative Writers and Day-Dreaming": the relation between creativity and the unconscious. What might be described as a neurosis in an analysand becomes for the writer a source of expression for fictive materials. Furthermore, we may detect in this attitude the notion that Nabokov's introductions, being nonfiction, are "reliable" texts upon which to base psychoanalytic formulation, while the novels, in their fictionality, might as well be off limits to interpretation. Nabokov, however, did not draw such a convenient demarcation between fiction and reality. When asked about his propensity for giving interviews, he replied, "What I really like about the better kind of public colloquy is the opportunity it affords me to construct in the presence of my audience the semblance of what I hope is a plausible and not altogether displeasing personality" (*Strong Opinions,* 158). Nabokov's public statements may thus be perceived as "constructions" put together with an audience in mind. The problem is: how are we to distinguish the overtly fictional constructions from the covertly fictional ones? Or, to put it another way, when is an author *not* contriving an image of authorship by writing?

The idea that psychoanalysis is to be resisted because "Nabokov would have wanted it that way," for instance, or because Nabokov demeaned all systems that he felt tended to falsify the nature of phenomena through excessive generalization or systematizing—such an idea is untenable for its dependence on the authorial intentionality of a text. Roland

Barthes's 1971 comments in "From Work to Text" are here pertinent: "It can be read without the guarantee of its father. . . . It is not that the Author may not 'come back' in the Text, in his text, but he then does so as a 'guest'. . . . He becomes, as it were, a paper-author: his life is no longer the origin of his fictions but a fiction contributing to his work" (*Image-Music-Text,* 161). What needs to be faced is the extent to which Nabokov's readers are reluctant to depart from the mode of reading he prescribed for them and to what degree this may be a perceived filial obligation.

I arrive at Freud and Nabokov not from an intrinsic irreverence, but from a desire to illuminate the manner in which they have come to be associated. I believe that Freud's writings are crucial to the nature of contemporary meaning. But the importance of Freud's work is not dependent on an overly restrictive conception of psychoanalysis or on the reductive propensities that all too often characterized the popularization of psychoanalysis in America after Freud's death. Freud's work constitutes a hermeneutical system of meaning, a conceptualization that both shapes and coexists with culture. In his perceptive essay, "The Question of Proof in Freud's Psychoanalytic Writings," Paul Ricoeur answered the persistent attacks that psychoanalysis was not scientifically verifiable: "If analytic experience is desire coming to discourse, the sort of truth that best answers to it is that of a saying-true rather than a being-true. . . . The truth claim of psychoanalysis can legitimately be placed within the field of intersubjective communication" (*Hermeneutics and the Human Sciences,* 265).

4

Understanding occurs—in both psychoanalysis and literature—through narrative: by telling we arrive at meaning. To experience is to know, but to form or hear or read a narrative is an experience as well. Psychoanalysis is both a telling and a doing: a subjective as well as objective enterprise. Proof must be determined in relation to both poles, much as we consider the validity of any interpretation.

At the same time that I affirm Freud, I assert the unique importance of Vladimir Nabokov. With Borges and Beckett he forms a triad that has changed the way we think about literature—and about life. The interdependence of fiction and life, the subjectivity and creativity that underlie our existence: all of this proceeds from Nabokov's writing. Alfred Kazin notes that "what moves us, indeed, is fiction *as* Nabokov's reality, the insistency of the emotional loyalties that his elaborate wary mind likes to conceal" (*Bright Book of Life,* 310).

Much of the excitement about psychoanalysis in contemporary critical theory has focused on the "return to Freud": the ability to perceive him subjectively as a writer in new and stimulating ways without being reined in by the restrictions of a codified theory of meaning; or, the freedom to *reconstruct* (in both a literary and psychoanalytical way) that system of meaning anew. According to Freud, it is the analyst's (or any interpreter's) "task . . . to make out what has been forgotten from the traces which it has left behind or, more correctly, to *construct* it" ("Constructions in Analysis," 258–59). Meaning so constituted is dependent on the context, or frame. Here Jacques Derrida acutely notes that "the structure of the framing effects is such that no totalization of the border is even possible. The frames are always framed" ("The Purveyer of Truth," 99). Narrative engenders narrative, resulting in a saying-true.

What is evident to me is that an analogous "return to Nabokov" would be desirable for us in order to appreciate Nabokov as a writer without being reined in by the restrictions he ordained as to how his work ought to be interpreted. For it seems increasingly clear that Nabokov's commentary on his work—his critical introductions, interviews, essays, even his posthumous lectures—must be read as a text created by an author whose intention was "to construct in the presence of [an] audience the semblance of . . . personality."

The meeting place for Freud and Nabokov is their shared enterprise of writing. In exploring two writers I hope to suggest the way in which psychoanalysis, as exemplified by Freud, has become more subjective and literary, subject to critical interpretation, while fiction, as exemplified by Nabokov, has become more theoretical.

The Writer and the World

In a 1971 interview, Nabokov was asked to explain his statement that "in a first-rate work of fiction, the real clash isn't between the characters, but between the author and the world." The novelist's answer was, "I believe I said 'between the author and the reader,' not 'the world,' which would be a meaningless formula, since a creative artist makes his own world or worlds. He clashes with readerdom because he is his own ideal reader and those other readers are so very often mere lip-moving ghosts and amnesiacs" (*Strong Opinions,* 183). But the interviewer's quotation was correct as originally stated. It appears in the revised 1966 version of Nabokov's autobiography, *Speak, Memory,* on page 290. In the first instance, the point was to refute the mimetic dependence of the novel on the world. In Nabokov's revision of his own statement, the modification describes an adversary relationship between writer and reader.

When a reader becomes involved with a novel's world, he or she agrees temporarily to suspend disbelief, to make of the fictional world an actual world for the duration of reading. Nabokov's original statement (which, aptly enough, was part of a metaphorical discussion of creativity in the composition of chess problems) assaults the premise of that tacit agreement. The clash is not between characters (as it would be between people in the real world) since characters are the mere fabrications of their creator, the author. The world in which the characters dwell—the novel—is a competitive world, a recasting of the possibilities of life. The author's inner or imaginary world—the novel—is in a clash with the outer or actual world. When we read a Nabokov novel, we are never to forget that the fictional world is different from the actual world, or that it was created by a specific author, Nabokov. As he stipulated in a 1964 interview, "A creative writer must study carefully the works of his rivals, including the Almighty. He must possess the inborn capacity not only of recombining but of re-creating the given world" (*Strong Opinions,* 32).

The clash between writer and world underscores the intentions lurking behind an author's work. When asked about his audience in 1962, Nabokov announced, "I don't think that an artist should bother about his audience. His best audience is the person he sees in his shaving mirror every morning. I think that the audience an artist imagines, when he imagines that kind of a thing, is a room filled with people wearing his own mask" (*Strong Opinions,* 18). Writing is a reproduction of the self, a doubling of the artist, an outward projection of an internal conception.

In a 1925 letter to Marie Bonaparte, Freud reached a similar conclusion: "No one writes to achieve fame, which anyhow is a very transitory matter, or the illusion of immortality. Surely we write first of all to satisfy something within ourselves, not for other people. Of course when others recognize one's efforts it increases the inner gratification, but nevertheless we write in the first place for ourselves, following an inner impulse" (Jones, 2, 397).

One reason for this affirmation of the writer as his own best audience may be the fact that, for a significant portion of their lives, the works of Freud and Nabokov were considered outre—outside the bounds of propriety—in terms of both subject matter and style. Freud's daring use of his own dreams as material in *The Interpretation of Dreams* (1900), as well as his emphasis on repressed erotic drives and the unconscious, resulted in his work being labeled unconventional and indecent. Nabokov's use of grotesque and violent materials combined with a singleminded dedication to a poetic style that flaunted the social realistic conventions of his day placed him, as well, on the periphery. With the world in apparent antagonism to the writer, it is no surprise that the center of creative activity focuses on "an inner impulse."

But Freud's sense of the writer is more primarily related to Nabokov's—through the concept of transference. To accept naively the clash of characters in a novel is to proclaim that the fictive is real: there is no difference between the novel and the world. In psychoanalytic discourse, the analysand will "suspend disbelief" and project onto the analyst the traits and qualities associated with other people from the past. But the crucial factor is the ability to differentiate between the transference and reality: "The danger of these states of transference evidently lies in the patient's misunderstanding their nature and taking them for fresh real experiences instead of reflections of the past" (*Outline of Psycho-Analysis*, 176). To accept naively the clash of analyst and analysand in psychoanalysis is to proclaim in a related sense that the fictive is real: psychoanalysis is taken *for* life instead of as a means by which we interpret life. Nabokov's statement proclaimed "there is an author behind that fictive world." Freud's intent is to delineate the author behind the fictive world of transference dynamics: "It is the analyst's task constantly to tear the patient out of his menacing illusion and to show him again and again that what he takes to be new real life is a reflection of the past" (*Outline of Psycho-Analysis*, 177). What the reader/analysand takes to be "new real life" in the novel/analysis is a "reflection of the past," authored by another. The analyst is not the "author" of my anger, love, etc.—it's my parent, sibling, etc., who is responsible. What you take as your world—"the" world—in that novel's clash of characters is not your world, Nabokov says, it's mine.

Once we grant the distinction between the writer and the world, we must ask why Nabokov modified his own words to reconstruct the clash as being "between the author and the reader." The clash occurs, Nabokov noted, because the writer is "his own ideal reader" while the readers are "lip-moving ghosts." If I, the writer, am the author, then why do I conceive of the reader (whom I imagine as wearing my own mask) as my adversary? Why do I, being me, resent the part of me that is not me?

The working of the transference in psychoanalysis and literature is still more pervasive. The reader of the text is in an analogous position to the analysand in the sense of developing a transference toward the text (which is based, like psychoanalysis, on a combination of what transpired in the reading and what associations from the past were brought to bear on the reading). But to the extent that the reader seeks critical meaning from the text, the reader is in an analogous position to the psychoanalyst. Shoshana Felman expresses this well: "With respect to the text, the literary critic occupies thus at once the place of the psychoanalyst (in the relation of interpretation) *and* the place of the patient (in the relation of transference)" ("To Open the Question," 55/56, 7).

To be both writer and nonwriter, or reader, is to be one self comprised of two—adversarial, *ambivalent*. According to Freud, the "transference is *ambivalent:* it comprises positive (affectionate) as well as negative (hostile) attitudes towards the analyst" (*Outline,* 175). And of course, the analyst may be subject to a countertransference toward the analysand. That Nabokov intuitively realized the parallel between the role of the analyst and the role of the author is evidenced by his 1964 comments that he daily interprets his dreams without resorting to the ideas of "the Viennese quack." "I urge my potential patients to do likewise" (*Strong Opinions,* 47).

And herein resides the ambivalence: Freud late in life issued a warning that "the analyst should respect [the analysand's] individuality" (*Outline,* 175). Despite Nabokov's insistence that he had "no social purpose, no moral message . . . no general ideas to exploit" (*Strong Opinions,* 16), it was nevertheless inevitable that he view the enterprise of writing as being a clash, not only between the author and the world but between the author and the reader: the (writing)

11

self who I am is somehow situated against the (reading) self who wears my mask. Why? Because that self is me and yet not me. Thus the reader as patient, as lip-moving ghost, as masked double of the self. And the positive side of the transference? "I have the greatest readers any author has ever had" (*Strong Opinions*, 192).

The act of writing (and of envisioning the reading of that writing) naturally encompasses a doubling so that Freud and Nabokov share a common ground. What Freud expressed about the analysand/patient may just as aptly apply to the reader: "What we want to hear from our patient is not only what he knows and conceals from other people; he is to tell us too what he does *not* know" (*Outline*, 174).

*R*epression: "The Return of Chorb"

"Freud's therapy was plainly the creation of a man who loved language and was exceptionally sensitive to words, nuances, overtones. He loved to read—and read between the lines." So noted Walter Kaufmann in his eloquent *Discovering the Mind* (vol. 3, 149). Freud's linguistic orientation is apparent in the 1909 lectures he gave at Clark University. In order to remove a symptom, he said, "it was necessary to reproduce the whole chain of pathogenic memories in chronological order, or rather in reversed order, the latest ones first and the earliest ones last" (*Five Lectures on Psycho-Analysis*, 14). Freud describes here a sequence, a following-back, a step-by-step retroactive reassembling of what is not perceived to exist but in fact already was. Discovery is thus a return. This idea is evident in Freud's 1905 *Three Essays on Sexuality:* "The finding of an object is in fact a refinding of it" (222).

Problems arise when an individual—despite the previous effects of the past—is unable to realize the present-ness of the past, unable to discern the chain of associations that tether the now to the before. Neurotics, Freud explained, "cannot get free of the past and for its sake they neglect what is real and immediate. This fixation of mental life to pathogenic traumas is one of the most significant and practically important characteristics of neurosis" (*Five Lectures,* 17).

Freud undoubtedly had no idea that a story would appear in his lifetime, published in Berlin (but in Russian, however!), that would embody many of these concepts. Not deliberately, of course, for its author cultivated as an *idée fixe* an abhorrence of psychoanalysis, but rather, the way Freud noted that an analysand who does not remember may yet convey: the analysand (or the fiction) "*acts* it out . . . reproduces it not as a memory but as an action" ("Remembering, Repeating, and Working Through," 150).

In "The Return of Chorb," a young newlywed returns as a widower to the small German town in which he was married. His wife had perished on their honeymoon by touching inadvertently a live wire: "Nothing, it seemed to him, could be purer than such a death, caused by the impact of an electric stream, the same stream which, when poured into glass receptacles, yields the purest and brightest light." Following his wife's death, Chorb experiences an abrupt withdrawal of libido from the world; he is unable even to attend his wife's funeral. "Chorb's entire world ceased to sound like a world: it retreated at once" (*Details of a Sunset,* 60).

The town is funereal, deathly, like the underworld, like the unconscious. Appropriately, "one could make out" through the window of his seedy hotel "in the velvety depths . . . a stone Orpheus outlined against the blue of the night" (*Details of a Sunset,* 68). Orpheus, too, had lost his wife, Eurydice, immediately following his wedding. But though he braved the underworld to save her, he was unable to resist his urge to look back upon her while she was still in death's cavern and the darkness reclaimed her. Orpheus was prevented from journeying twice into the world of the dead. Chorb, then, wishes to do what Orpheus was unable to do—rescue his wife from the dead. But in this case, the dead realm is the world of the unconscious.

How does psychoanalysis enable a modern Orpheus to descend for a second time into the underworld? Freud stipulates that "in order to bring about recovery, the symptom must be led back along the same paths and once more turned into the repressed idea" (*Five Lectures,* 27). Paths of the mind that are dead to memory, but also, for Chorb, the paths of a world that is dead without the investment of libido.

Chorb's behavior attests to his desire to undo his wife's death. As a result of his defensive mechanisms, "he had returned alone from abroad and only now realized that, like it or not, he would have to explain how his wife had perished, and why he had written nothing about it to his in-laws."

Nevertheless, on his appearance at his in-laws' home, he is unable to leave a message with the maid concerning his wife's death. He tells her instead "that their daughter was ill . . . only because it was easier to utter" (*Details of a Sunset*, 60). It is no accident that the parents are away attending Wagner's *Parsifal,* the work of a composer whose dreamy love of death evokes the spirit of Chorb's struggle.

Before arriving at the town of his wife's parents, Chorb "passed in reverse through all the spots they had visited together during their honeymoon journey" (*Details of a Sunset,* 61), demonstrating Freud's contention that "an obsessive or compulsive thought is one whose function it is to represent an act regressively" ("Notes upon a Case of Obsessional Neurosis," 246). He had been unable to contact his wife's parents because "he wished to possess his grief all by himself, without tainting it by any foreign substance and without sharing it with any other soul" (*Details of a Sunset,* 60).

Chorb expresses the intention behind his backward journey as follows: "He thought that if he managed to gather all the little things they had noticed together—if he recreated thus the near past—her image would grow immortal and replace her for ever" (*Details of a Sunset,* 61). He wants "her image" to replace "her"; he desires a living "image" to substitute for the dead person. In town his reverse honeymoon is nearly completed; there is only the retracing of the first night he and his wife had spent together, in the same seedy hotel that he now occupies. "Thus Chorb traveled back to the very source of his recollections, an agonizing and yet blissful test now drawing to a close. All there remained was but a single night to be spent in that first chamber of their marriage, and by tomorrow the test would be passed and her image perfect" (*Details of a Sunset,* 66).

After revealing his hotel and conveying the misleading message that his wife was ill, Chorb "suddenly understood that, despite exhaustion, he would not be able to sleep alone in that room with its naked bulb and whispery crannies" (*Details of a Sunset,* 66). Like Orpheus before him, he requires a visual image of life, not realizing that to look upon that which is dead kills the possibility of its life. Thus he hires a prostitute to occupy his wife's space in the hotel room, to be a substitute for his wife's presence. But according to Freud, "*The repressed wishful impulse continues to exist in the unconscious.* It is on the look-out for an opportunity of being activated, and when that happens it succeeds in sending into consciousness a disguised and unrecognizable *substitute* for what had been repressed, and to this there soon become attached the same feelings of unpleasure which it was hoped had been saved by the repression" (*Five Lectures,* 27).

The sleep of Chorb and the prostitute is disturbed by "Chorb screaming. He had awakened some time after midnight, had turned on his side and had seen his wife lying beside him." Chorb screams "horribly" as he watches "the white specter of a woman" leap from the bed; but does he scream because this is the prostitute, or because his dead Eurydice has come back to life? "Slowly [he] recognized the girl . . . [and] heaved a sigh of relief for he realized that the ordeal was over" (*Details of a Sunset,* 68–69).

But is it over? "The crux of the matter," Freud wrote in one of his last articles, "is that the defensive mechanisms directed against former danger recur in the treatment as *resistances* against recovery. It follows from this that the ego treats recovery itself as a new danger" ("Analysis Terminable and Interminable," 238). Why did Orpheus look back, defying the gods, and thus kill the possibility of Eurydice's returning to life? Why did Chorb leave the message that his wife was merely ill? Why had he been unable to sleep without the prostitute in his room?

Arriving home late from the opera and hearing that their daughter is ill and in town, the parents rush to the seedy hotel. The desk clerk tries to alert them that "a lady" is in the room with Chorb, just as the father insists "she's my daughter." The door opens, and the clerk and prostitute rush out, the parents enter, the door shuts and . . . but what else could occur? By seizing on the substitute, the visual image, Chorb has destroyed the purity of his wife's death. Instead of the original (repressed) image to replace her, there is now a new image: of her two parents, Chorb, and a prostitute.

Chorb has been unable to establish the sequence, the necessary chain of memories needed to bring to life the image of his wife; as a result, like Eurydice, she dies a second death. According to Freud, "In the many different forms of obsessional neurosis in particular, forgetting is mostly restricted to dissolving thought connections, failing to draw the right conclusions and isolating memories" ("Remembering, Repeating, and Working Through," 149). And what remains for Chorb? "In the room all was silence" (*Details of a Sunset,* 70).

*T*he Ideal Fiction

The philosopher Walter Kaufmann, in his book on Freud, concluded that "one simply cannot describe fully everything that was the case. Every description involves interpretations, and all understanding and explaining depend on selection" (*Discovering the Mind*, 3, 281). What has occurred may not be fully described or chronicled: a creation with words is a re-creation. The extent to which we possess subjective sensibilities restricts our ability to see anything but a partial view. Thus, selection—what is included or omitted in a written account—is close to artistic arrangement, a stylistic choice or tactic for presentation.

Jacques Derrida has referred with acuity to "the open letter, the very open letter, which fiction is" ("The Purveyer of Truth," 64). And in fact all writing—depending as it does on selection, arrangement, individual interpretation—must necessarily be open to a multitude of interpretive possibilities, truths, strategies of meaning. This not only applies to literary art but to the artistic component in the endeavor of psychoanalysis. According to psychoanalyst Roy Schafer, psychoanalytic case histories, "over which analysts have labored so hard, may now be seen in a new light: less as positivistic sets of factual findings about mental development and more as hermeneutically filled-in narrative structures" ("Narration in the Psychoanalytic Dialogue," 53).

But announcing a narrative basis for psychoanalysis is a

far cry from announcing its demise (as commentators such as Frederick Crews have been all too eager to proclaim). Indeed, Freud noted as early as *The Interpretation of Dreams* that "just as all neurotic symptoms, and, for that matter, dreams, are capable of being 'over-interpreted' and indeed need to be, if they are to be fully understood, so all genuinely creative writings are the product of more than a single motive and more than a single impulse in the poet's mind, and are open to more than a single interpretation" (266).

Although it is my impression that Nabokov was not aware of Freud's willingness to allow for "more than a single interpretation" (he conceived of Freud as a demonic monomaniacal champion of one interpretation for all situations), it is doubtful that the concept of overinterpretation would have made a significant difference to his conception of psychoanalysis. "I do not believe in *any* kind of 'interpretation' so that his or my 'interpretation' can be neither a failure nor a success" (*Strong Opinions,* 263). Rather than the play of meaning, the free play of signifiers, Nabokov insists on the sole integrity of the artistic thing-in-itself. "The book I make is a subjective and specific affair" (*Strong Opinions,* 115).

Nabokov's suspicion was of the general formulation, the pigeonhole into which precise sensations were to be indiscriminately inserted. He insisted that "at a time when American readers are taught from high school on to seek in books 'general ideas' a critic's duty should be to draw their attention to the specific detail, to the unique image, without which . . . there can be no art, no genius, no Chekhov, no terror, no tenderness, and no surprise" (*The Nabokov-Wilson Letters,* 298). But what principle of selection or aesthetics of arrangement would dictate which "specific details" were to be examined and which ignored? Is there not a "general idea" of interpretation behind an adherence to no general ideas?

Freud's realization that neurotic symptoms, dreams, and literature all necessitate overinterpretation was not confined to the way in which psychoanalysis proceeds. He recognized that the structuring concepts of psychoanalysis—its system of classifying and understanding—were, like all meaning systems, reductive and inadequate in the face of the variety of phenomena. "A normal ego . . . is, like normality in general, an ideal fiction. . . . Every normal person, in fact, is only normal on the average. His ego approximates to that of the psychotic in some part or other and to a greater or lesser extent" ("Analysis Terminable and Interminable," 235). It is precisely this recognition on Freud's part that gives psychoanalysis such strength and richness. If normality is "an ideal fiction," so, too, are the concepts of past and present. My life (as I come to understand it through psychoanalysis) is a specific narrative part of all lives. By distinguishing between the ideal and the practical, meaningful associations are established between inner and outer reality, the self and the world, life and fiction. An illustration may be provided in Roy Schafer's statement that "more and more, the alleged past must be experienced consciously as a mutual interpenetration of the past and present, both being viewed in psychoanalytically organized and coordinated terms" ("Narration in the Psychoanalytic Dialogue," 36).

Nabokov would never agree to the general idea that normality is a fiction and that all thinking contains elements of madness, but in fact, his fiction is centered on precisely this notion. Describing himself, he suggested that "looking at it objectively, I have never seen a more lucid, more lonely, better balanced mad mind than mine" (*Strong Opinions,* 129). It was when he was faced with the *distinction* between himself and his characters that he struggled to erect fences, ideal fictions of self and other, in order to "construct in the presence of my audience the semblance of what I hope is a plausible and not altogether displeasing personality" (*Strong Opinions,* 158).

Describing himself in an interview, Nabokov worked to construct an ideal fiction of normality that he would exploit repeatedly in subsequent interviews: "I don't belong to any club or group. I don't fish, cook, dance, endorse books, sign books, co-sign declarations, eat oysters, get drunk, go to church, go to analysts, or take part in demonstrations" (*Strong Opinions,* 18). I am not taking issue with the truth of these statements but rather with the principle of selection that I see working: the author as supreme individualist, the author of dreary normalcy. Certainly Nabokov had the right to protect his private life, but rarely in modern literature can we find an example of an author so zealously and frequently commenting in interviews on a private life that he believes to be uninteresting.

When queried in the same interview as to whether his characters are perverse, his response was "Maybe. Some of my characters are, no doubt, pretty beastly, but I really don't care, they are outside my inner self like the mournful monsters of a cathedral façade—demons placed there merely to show that they have been booted out." This is tantamount to a holding-off of his characters: perhaps my characters are "pretty beastly," but they're not me; they're "outside my inner self," a mere external façade that is part of art and not real as I am. Nabokov insisted that he was "a mild old gentleman who loathe[d] cruelty" (*Strong Opinions,* 19), whose artistic "notions of strategy" were "deceit, to the point of diabolism, and originality, verging upon the grotesque" (*Speak, Memory,* 289), an author who was "very careful to keep [his] characters beyond the limits of [his] own identity" (*Strong Opinions,* 13).

Nabokov associated art with genius, terror, tenderness, and surprise. A reader is informed by "the tingle in the spine" (*Strong Opinions,* 41) about the quality of a novel. But when constructing the fiction of his public personality through his interviews, Nabokov seized on what Freud described as the "ideal fiction": "a normal ego," in dreary opposition to the brilliant inventiveness of his novels. Despite the remarkable openness of meaning in the novels, Nabokov's public persona struggles to achieve (in opposition to Derrida's phrase) a closed letter of meaning and interpretation. Think of the novel as old-fashioned case history: I am merely reporting the specific clinical findings, but other than my scientific role, I have nothing to do with this case. Oh, really?

When asked in an interview what his position was in the world of letters, Nabokov replied, "Jolly good view from up here" (*Strong Opinions,* 181). Undoubtedly, his response was based on his assessment of his accomplishment as a novelist. In effect, however, he is asserting: I am my novels, but I am not *of* them. The praise and approval of the audience is appreciated and deserved but the novelist remains unconnected to the materials of his novels: they are on the outside, "mournful monsters," while his "inner self" is safe, normal, and concealed. Is this an ideal fiction?

Nabokov worked very hard on each of *his* volumes. Nevertheless, he mused that "what I would welcome at the close of a book of mine is a sensation of its world receding in the distance and stopping somewhere there, suspended afar like a picture in a picture" (*Strong Opinions,* 72–73).

Out there, suspended out there, but not in here, where I am. . . .

*R*eality: My Place or Yours?

When asked in an interview whether he found anything Proustian in his own "concern for memory" and his "recollection of personal detail," Nabokov replied: "I see no resemblance whatever. Proust *imagined* a person . . . who had a Bergsonian concept of past time. . . . I am *not* an imaginary person and my memories are direct rays deliberately trained, not sparks and spangles" (Gerald Clarke, "Checking In with Vladimir Nabokov," 69). Nabokov's insistence on his own substantiality (as opposed to fictionality) is borne out by the initial title for his autobiography, *Conclusive Evidence:* "conclusive evidence of my having existed" (*Speak, Memory,* 11). Indeed, while working on his memoir, Nabokov wrote to Edmund Wilson that he had in mind "a new type of autobiography—a scientific attempt to unravel and trace back all the tangled threads of one's personality" (*The Nabokov-Wilson Letters,* 188).

It is provocative that Nabokov would refer to his autobiography as "scientific," and as a "systematically correlated assemblage of personal recollections" (*Speak, Memory,* 9)—and nevertheless publish two chapters of this "conclusive evidence" of his existence ("First Love" and "Mademoiselle O") in his *Nabokov's Dozen* as fiction! Does this indicate that Nabokov wished to blur the distinction between real and imaginary existence? Au contraire: for in 1967 he wrote the *London Times* to correct an account given there of his father's murder. "I wish to submit," he noted, "that at a time when in so many eastern countries history has become a joke, this precise beam of light upon a precious detail may be of some help to the next investigator" (*Strong Opinions,* 215). Again that year he wrote to *Encounter* to mock the appearance of the highly speculative Freud-Bullitt collaboration on Woodrow Wilson, citing its "comic appeal." And in 1971, he wrote to the *New York Times* to protest the account of him presented in Edmund Wilson's memoir, *Upstate,* "in which living persons are but the performing poodles of the diarist's act" (*Strong Opinions,* 219).

Reality, for Nabokov, "is a very subjective affair" that allows selective autobiographical accounts to pass as fiction and yet obliges errors and distortions to be corrected scrupulously. "You can get nearer and nearer, so to speak, to reality; but you never get near enough because reality is an infinite succession of steps, levels of perception, false bottoms, and hence unquenchable, unattainable. You can know more and more about one thing but you can never know everything about one thing: it's hopeless" (*Strong Opinions,* 10–11). Hence Nabokov may feel able to correct misinformation about his father's death or write an autobiography because he knows "more and more" about "one thing"—his existence. Having established, in effect, that all reality is subjective, Nabokov functions *as if* his version of reality is real while other versions are fictional. And this is precisely why *Speak, Memory* is so moving and compelling: the arbitrariness of reality renders the truth of the account in the telling—words *and* worlds depend on how the narrative is presented, arranged, displayed. "What I feel to be the real modern world is the world the artist creates, his own mirage, which becomes a new *mir* ('world' in Russian) by the very act of his shedding, as it were, the age he lives in" (*Strong Opinions,* 112). Nabokov's autobiography becomes "conclusive evidence" not because of its necessarily subjective limitation but because the memoirist knows "more and more" about that subjectivity through the act of writing it, and the written account itself has bulk, substantiality—it sheds the competing account of history.

Freud was similarly skeptical about the likelihood of attaining an objective rendering of reality. Writing in 1936 to dissuade Arnold Zweig from attempting a biography, Freud wrote: "Whoever undertakes to write a biography binds himself to lying, to concealment, to hypocrisy, to flummery and even to hiding his own lack of understanding, since biographical material is not to be had and if it were it could not be used. Truth is not accessible; mankind does not deserve it" (Jones, 3, 208). (It is a Nabokovian irony that the text of Freud's antibiography statement appears in Ernest Jones's biography of Freud!)

In his last work, *An Outline of Psycho-Analysis,* Freud expanded his conclusion on biography to include reality: "We have no hope of being able to reach [the real state of affairs] itself, since it is evident that everything new that we have inferred must nevertheless be translated back into the language of our perceptions, from which it is simply impossible for us to free ourselves. . . . Reality will always remain 'unknowable'" (196). But this did not prevent Freud from conjecturing (in the very same book) that Shakespeare's works were written by the Earl of Oxford (192)! How did Freud bridge the gap between an "unknowable reality" and the willingness to speculate on the life of Moses, for instance, in his *Moses and Monotheism?* For Freud, like Nabokov, it was necessary to mediate between the impracticality of knowing reality and the urgency of knowing something in some way. "The yield," he suggested in that last work, "will consist in an insight into connections and dependent relations which are present in the external world, which can somehow be reliably reproduced or reflected in the internal world of our thought"

(196). We may never know, but we gain "insight into connections and dependent relations"; what we gain insight about in the "external world" may "somehow" be "reliably reproduced or reflected in the internal world."

For Freud, reality remains unknowable outside of our subjective perception of it, but even so, insights may be derived that enable us to make connections between the internal world and the external world. These psychoanalytical insights are related crucially to the "language of our perceptions"; it is "impossible for us to free ourselves" from the perceptual basis of our psychoanalytic knowledge. Thus we are a part of what we observe; our perspective defines what we perceive. The account we provide of what we know is also an account of how we came to provide the account: is it any wonder that Freud utilized his own dreams in *The Interpretation of Dreams?*

"We shall never know," Nabokov believed, "the origin of life, or the meaning of life, or the nature of space and time, or the nature of nature, or the nature of thought" (*Strong Opinions,* 45). And because we shall never know (in any ultimate sense), what we do create of our knowing (in the form of writing) is both a fiction and a reality: a fiction because we may only approach reality, and a reality because the act of writing, the process of forming a "systematically correlated assemblage" of words or memories, is a way of knowing "more and more," or, in Freud's words, of gaining "insight into connections and dependent relations."

Despite the impossibility of knowing, we agree to allow

interpretations to take on the qualities of knowledge. According to psychoanalyst Donald P. Spence, "Once a given construction has acquired narrative truth, it becomes just as real as any other kind of truth; this new reality becomes a significant part of the psychoanalytic cure" (*Narrative Truth and Historical Truth,* 31). What we agree to know is derived from our constructions, our interpretations, the stories we tell. So when Vladimir Nabokov confessed, "I am an ardent memoirist with a rotten memory," he was providing the reason why *Speak, Memory* is both truth and fiction: "With absolute lucidity I recall landscapes, gestures, intonations, a million sensuous details, but names and numbers topple into oblivion" (*Strong Opinions,* 140).

But it is difficult to live in a world of unknowable reality. The tendency is to grant the point and then retreat into either fiction or reality. A good deal of the profundity and importance of psychoanalysis is that it situates itself in the realm of the "saying-true" rather than the "being-true." This is not an easy place to be, however. To derive meaning from narrative, to be fictive and yet true, is to exist in a realm without convenient limits. What I construct or write is me and also something other than me. It is not reality as an absolute, but as a place: the place of inner sensation, or the external form I provide it through words. My place or yours? Nabokov's formulation is no less acute:

> I have often noticed that after I had bestowed on the characters of my novels some treasured item of my past, it would pine away in the artificial world where I

28

had so abruptly placed it. Although it lingered on in my mind, its personal warmth, its retrospective appeal had gone and, presently, it became more closely identified with my novel than with my former self, where it had seemed to be so safe from the intrusion of the artist. . . . The man in me revolts against the fictionist. (*Speak, Memory,* 95)

*W*ho's in Charge Here?

In the foreword to his book of interviews, Nabokov stipulated the three "absolute conditions" under which he would agree to conduct an interview: "The interviewer's questions have to be sent to me in writing, answered by me in writing, and reproduced verbatim." His reason for insisting on these conditions is: "I think like a genius, I write like a distinguished author, and I speak like a child." Oral communication falls short of the specificity of written communication (which has an implied object—the reader—whom Nabokov conceives in his own image), and significantly short of one's private thoughts (which are not intended to be communicated). Nabokov rejected the aspects of the literary interview that were dependent on human interaction: "But the interviewer wishes to visit me. He wishes to see my pencil poised above the page, my painted lampshade, my bookshelves. . . . Have I the heart to cancel the cosiness? I have." In preparing the interviews for publication, Nabokov was pleased to leave out the "well-meant little touches" and the "gaudiest journalistic inventions" that departed from the "basic substance" of the written text. His goal was to "gradually eliminat[e] every element of spontaneity, all semblance of actual talk. The thing is transmuted finally into a more or less neatly paragraphed essay, and that is the ideal form a written interview should take" (*Strong Opinions,* ix–x).

Considering Nabokov's attitude about interviews, it is worth wondering why he granted them. His answer: "My fiction allows me so seldom the occasion to air my private views that I rather welcome, now and then, the questions put to me in sudden spates by charming, courteous, intelligent visitors" (*Strong Opinions,* x). There are two points worth noting here: first, Nabokov felt that his fiction did not provide him "the occasion to air [his] private views"; and even in the abstract, Nabokov was at work creating a picture of the ideal interviewer (an image of himself?): "charming, courteous, intelligent."

Despite Nabokov's announced intention of "gradually eliminating every element of spontaneity," his answer to a question about his "principal failing as a writer" was "lack of spontaneity; the nuisance of parallel thoughts, second thoughts, third thoughts; inability to express myself properly in any language unless I compose every damned sentence in my bath, in my mind, at my desk" (*Strong Opinions,* 34). Nabokov's stated conditions are proclaimed boldly in his preface. Nevertheless, there is the sense here that, much as he would like to be spontaneous, he is *obliged* to be controlling in order to express himself "properly." For Nabokov, the literary interview leaves out "all semblance of actual talk." Spontaneous speech has been transformed into premeditated writing: the interview becomes entirely the creation of its author.

With such a pronounced emphasis on contrivance, it is striking to find Nabokov announcing (in the same interview) his "political creed": "freedom of speech, freedom of thought, freedom of art" (*Strong Opinions,* 34–35). In this sense, *free* has little similarity to *spontaneous*. "Freedom of speech" must be understood to mean "freedom of writing," since for Nabokov speech freely spoken must be transformed into carefully controlled written discourse. In a 1968 interview, he even includes his directions to the interviewer as a preface to the text: "I like to see the proofs for checking last-minute misprints or possible little flaws of fact. . . . I would like the stuff I prepared in typescript to be presented as direct speech on my part, whilst other statements which I may stammer out in the course of our chats, and the gist of which you might want to incorporate in The Profile, should be used, please, obliquely or paraphrastically, without any quotes" (*Strong Opinions,* 108). These "requests" are, in fact, elaborate directions for the creation of a "live" interview from out of a written exchange of letters. But lest the reader resent the illusion of spontaneity, Nabokov proclaims the contrivance, reminding us constantly that the form has been prescribed by him.

Why do we find this meticulous attention to interviews? After all, Nabokov indicated in his last interview that "the reader has no business bothering about the author's intentions, nor has the author any business trying to learn whether the consumer likes what he consumes" (*Vladimir Nabokov: A Tribute,* 122). Writing about Freud, Donald P. Spence noted that "if we followed what Freud says in his writings, we would find ourselves looking for historical truth. . . . On the other hand, if we look at what Freud does, at how he writes, how he interprets, and how he assembles his explanations, we see the strong influence of the narrative tradition and we learn from him the clinical importance of narrative truth" (*Narrative Truth and Historical Truth,* 32). Similarly, if we follow what Nabokov says in his interviews, then we would conclude that he has no general purpose in granting them, or issuing them. But if we look at how he assembles his interviews, at how he "speaks" them, we discover an author who not only cares deeply whether the consumer likes his work but is trying to influence that reader's appraisal of it.

Nabokov's conception of his audience dictated his statement that "I write for myself in multiplicate." But if the reader is another version of me, why don't I assume that my reader will view my work as sympathetically as I do? If Nabokov's reader is a projection of himself, why the need to control so rigorously the form of the interview that the reader will see? In terms of his audience, Nabokov wanted it both ways: they are his "multiplicate," but he also issued decrees as to who might belong to the group. "Young dunces who turn to drugs cannot read *Lolita,* or any of my books" (*Strong Opinions,* 114). "My books . . . are addressed not to 'dunderheads'; not to the cretins who believe that I like long Latinate words; not to the learned loonies who find sexual or religious allegories in my fiction" (*Strong Opinions,* 196).

Nabokov's sympathetic reader threatens to change, at any moment, into an unfriendly critic. Needless to say, such a transformation would also encompass a modification of the self. For this reason, Nabokov feels obliged to describe his "advice" to any literary critic:

> Learn to distinguish banality. Remember that mediocrity thrives on "ideas." Beware of the modish message. Ask yourself if the symbol you have detected is not your own footprint. Ignore allegories. By all means place the "how" above the "what" but do not let it be confused with the "so what." Rely on the sudden erection of your small dorsal hairs. Do not drag in Freud at this point. All the rest depends on personal talent. (*Strong Opinions,* 66)

In effect, Nabokov's advice to his reader-critic is much like his directions to his interviewer: follow my instructions carefully and in every regard; the rest is up to you. But what else is there? What talent is then required? Nabokov had only one "favor" to ask of the "serious critic": "sufficient perceptiveness to understand that whatever term or trope I use, my purpose is not to be facetiously flashy or grotesquely obscure but to express what I feel and think with the utmost truthfulness and perception" (*Strong Opinions,* 179). In other words, if you see the truthfulness and perception in my work, then you are a serious critic, a Nabokov in multiplicate; if you find me flashy or obscure, then you are not serious and I do not take you seriously.

It is instructive to consider Spence's statement that "the problems faced by the writer are, in many ways, the problems faced by the patient. In parallel fashion, the problems of the reader—and particularly the critical reader—are those faced by the analyst" (*Narrative Truth and Historical Truth,* 41). The analysand is often very concerned about what the analyst will think. Freud notes, in fact, that the analysand "develops a special interest in the person of the doctor"—as a result of the transference (*Introductory Lectures on Psycho-Analysis,* 439). The analysand wants to be liked by the analyst, wants the analyst to read the text of his life (the text that emanates from his life) in a favorable way. As a result of the transference, the analysis proceeds swimmingly. "But such fine weather cannot last for ever. One day it clouds over. Difficulties arise in the treatment. . . . [The analysand] behaves as though he were outside the treatment" (*Introductory Lectures,* 440). A resistance appears, to the ordinary operation of the analysis, to the process of interpretive reading. The analysand resists "the process of *free association*—that is, to say whatever came into his head, while ceasing to give any conscious direction to his thoughts" (*An Autobiographical Study,* 40). And as a result, we have the gradual elimination of "every element of spontaneity, all semblance of actual talk." The author's reader becomes the image in the mirror.

*P*sychoanalyze Yourself

In 1926, Freud contributed a prefatory note to an article by E. Pickworth Farrow, "A Childhood Memory from the Sixth Month of Life." The article (and Freud's introduction) were then included in Farrow's *A Practical Method of Self-Analysis* (1942). By 1972 the title of the reprinted paperback edition had been changed to *Psychoanalyze Yourself*. Freud wrote:

> The author of this paper is known to me as a man of strong and independent intelligence. Probably through being somewhat self-willed he failed to get on to good terms with two analysts with whom he made the attempt. He thereupon proceeded to make a systematic application of the procedure of self-analysis which I myself employed in the past for the analysis of my own dreams. His findings deserve attention precisely on account of the peculiar character of his personality and of his technique. (280)

Certainly, it is no rare event for Freud to have issued an endorsement (albeit a qualified one); throughout his writings, we find frequent allusions to works and authors that he found noteworthy. But Freud's statement indicates that Farrow made "systematic application of the procedure of self-analysis which I myself employed in the past for the analysis of my own dreams." Thus, Farrow's practical method is thought by Freud to be comparable to his own method of self-analysis. Farrow's method, however, is a *written analysis:* "Write down on the paper whaatever comes into one's conscious mind at any given instant" (*Psychoanalyze Yourself,* 56).

The form of writing—in Farrow's case—facilitated his ability to conduct a self-analysis. Writing enabled him to transcribe "material which was very unpleasant to him so very much more easily and quickly in the first place by himself than he could tell it to an analyst." In fact, when Farrow tried "dictating free-associations to an electric recording and dictating machine in the hope that this method might work as well as writing . . . he found that this method was not having any therapeutic effect." By writing, Farrow was able to achieve an effective "otherness" that stimulated the process of free association; during dictation, he was inhibited by the sensation of his own voice which prompted the disturbing impression that "even walls have ears" (*Psychoanalyze Yourself,* 59–60).

Freud, in an 1897 letter to Wilhelm Fliess, wrote that "my self-analysis is still interrupted and I have realized the reason. I can only analyze myself with the help of knowledge obtained objectively (like an outsider). Genuine self-analysis is impossible" (*On the History of the Psycho-Analytic Movement,* 20–21). In a remarkable moment of insightful self-awareness, Freud realized that one must cultivate (or contrive) an objective self in order to come to know one's subjective self. One must be "like an outsider" in order to know what is inside.

The brilliance of Freud's achievement of self-analysis lay

precisely in his uncanny ability to view himself as two selves: the subjective self being analyzed, and an objective self conducting the analysis. But looking back on the process in 1935, Freud concluded that "in self-analysis the danger of incompleteness is particularly great. One is too soon satisfied with a part explanation, behind which resistance may easily be keeping back something that is more important perhaps" ("The Subtleties of a Faulty Action," 234). It is for this reason that Freud viewed self-analysis as being in the main less desirable than conventional psychoanalysis. But we now know that Freud's self-analysis was not conducted in a vacuum. It stimulated and was stimulated by his work on *The Interpretation of Dreams*. In addition, he described (as an outsider) his work of self-analysis in his letters to Fliess. Writing, for Freud as well as for Farrow, was integral to the process of self-analysis. Intrinsic to writing is the concept of the split between the written self and the self that reads. As one subjectively writes, one simultaneously contrives the image of an objective self that reads. Writing, therefore, encompasses a process of transference between these two embodiments of the self. (It is ironic that Farrow believed that transference was "quite unnecessary"; nevertheless, he did suggest that "the patient may himself be acting as a personal analyst" (*Psychoanalyze Yourself,* 16].)

Despite his aversion to psychoanalysis, it may be discerned that Nabokov was engaged in a self-analysis. "I take gleeful pleasure every morning," he noted, "in refuting the Viennese quack by recalling and explaining the details of my dreams without using one single reference to sexual symbols or mythical complexes" (*Strong Opinions,* 47). He read (with amusement) during the summer of 1956 Freud's letters to Fliess (*Nabokov-Wilson Letters,* 300). Moreover, he was well acquainted with the works of Havelock Ellis (Field, *Nabokov: His Life in Part,* 96). And in an interview, responding to a question as to whether he had ever "experienced hallucinations" (asked by James Mossman, not by Charles Kinbote!), he noted that he "often enjoy[ed] . . . a continuous series of extraordinary bright, fluidly changing pictures" and that "reports on those enigmatic phenomena can be found in the case histories collected by psychiatrists but no satisfying interpretation has come my way. Freudians, keep out, please" (*Strong Opinions,* 144–45).

It is my belief that through his interviews Nabokov was constructing a fictive version of himself: he crafted the image of himself in his interviews as he would a fictional character. In his last interview, he remarked, "If I do have any obsessions I'm careful not to reveal them in fictional form" (*Vladimir Nabokov: A Tribute,* 125). But Freud, in his *An Autobiographical Study,* maintained that "invented dreams can be interpreted in the same way as real ones and . . . the unconscious mechanisms familiar to us in the 'dream-work' are thus also operative in the processes of imaginative writing" (65). Writing was, for Nabokov, a method of self-analysis. In its duality, in the process of shaping a world by depicting it, he came to know himself as both a subjective and objective self. If writing constituted a form of self-analysis for Nabokov, then we may say, in the words of Freud, that "the patient does not *remember* anything of what he has forgotten and repressed, but *acts* it out. He reproduces it not as a memory but as an action; he *repeats* it, without, of course, knowing that he is repeating it" ("Remembering, Repeating and Working Through," 150).

In the first chapter of *Speak, Memory,* Nabokov describes how, while he was still a young boy, his father would be called away from meals to decide a matter for the peasants on the family estate, Vyra. When Nabokov's father granted the request, he would be tossed in the air by the peasants:

> Thrice, to the mighty heave-ho of his invisible tossers, he would fly up in this fashion, and the second time he would go higher than the first and then there he would be, on his last and loftiest flight, reclining, as if for good, against the cobalt blue of the summer noon, like one of those paradisiac personages who comfortably soar, with such a wealth of folds in their garments, on the vaulted ceiling of a church while below, one by one, the wax tapers in mortal hands light up to make a swarm of minute flames in the mist of incense, and the priest chants of eternal repose and funeral lilies conceal the face of whoever lies there, among the swimming lights, in the open coffin. (31–32)

Phyllis Roth, in her richly suggestive "Toward the Man behind the Mystification," rightly terms this a "proleptic reminiscence" that foreshadows the descriptions later in the book of the murder of Nabokov's father (54).

But, in addition, we have a description that begins as an

evocation of life's vitality and transforms itself into a scene of death. The adult recalling this memory from childhood has conflated the enjoyable youthful scene with the affect derived from the knowledge that his father would later be assassinated. It is as if the passage is animated by the process of condensation. The child's concern that something might happen to the father tossed in the air, combined with the ambivalence accompanying all childhood attitudes toward parents, is given expression by the later event (the murder) which, as yet, is unrevealed in the narrative. It is not unusual in a dream for the dreamer to have a sensation that does not coincide with the scene of the dream—"an intense expression of affect appears in connection with subject-matter which seems to provide no occasion for any such expression" (Freud, *Interpretation of Dreams,* 460). The life of the father for the son is integrally related to thoughts of his death. It is no accident that the chapter which ends with this scene begins with "the cradle rocks above an abyss . . . our existence is but a brief crack of light between two eternities of darkness" (19).

Nabokov's art has "reproduce[d]" the psychic reality of his father, "not as a memory but as an action." In that one scene of death-in-life, the two halves of the self are united in a poignant moment of written self-analysis.

*M*emory Equals Dream

In *Speak, Memory,* Nabokov envisioned a "delicate meeting place between imagination and knowledge"—between what we create and what exists—"that is intrinsically artistic" (167). He moved beyond this position in a 1967 interview when he asserted that "imagination is a form of memory. . . . An image depends on the power of association and association is supplied and prompted by memory. . . . In this sense, both memory and imagination are a negation of time" (*Strong Opinions,* 78). Thus, what we imagine is based on the associations provided by remembered experience. The past is revealed as one seamless artistic creation.

There is an indelible moment in *Speak, Memory* when Nabokov is unable to recall the name of Colette's dog. He relates other associative memories until "a delightful thing happens. The process of recreating [the other details] stimulates my memory to a last effort. I try again to recall the name of Colette's dog—and triumphantly, along those remote beaches, over the glossy evening sands of the past where each footprint slowly fills up with sunset water, here it comes, here it comes, echoing and vibrating: Floss, Floss, Floss!" (151–52). Once conceived, always a part of us: through the art of memory the past is brought together as a unity. Freud was no stranger to this attitude. He described for his 1909 Clark University audience how "when I reached a point with [my analysands] at which they maintained that they knew nothing more, I assured them that they *did* know it all the same, and that they had only to say it; and I ventured to declare that the right memory would occur to them at the moment at which I laid my hand on their forehead" (*Five Lectures,* 23).

Nabokov believed that "one is always at home in one's

past" (*Speak, Memory,* 116). Even supposed inaccuracies of recollection are actually valuable within the continuity of memory: "The distortion of a remembered image may not only enhance its beauty with an added refraction, but provide informative links with earlier or later patches of the past" (*Strong Opinions,* 143). Similarly, Freud found it "impossible to believe that an idea produced by a patient while his attention was on the stretch could be an arbitrary one and unrelated to the idea we were in search of" (*Five Lectures,* 29).

Referring, in *The Interpretation of Dreams,* to the work of an earlier researcher, Freud commented: "The way in which the memory behaves in dreams is undoubtedly of the greatest importance for any theory of memory in general. It teaches us that 'nothing which we have once mentally possessed can be entirely lost'" (20). Nabokov's refrain in *Speak, Memory* sounds a chord of agreement: "I witness with pleasure the supreme achievement of memory, which is the masterly use it makes of innate harmonies when gathering to its fold the suspended and wandering tonalities of the past" (170).

Nabokov believed in the process of memory as a creative endeavor by which life is recalled and transformed into art. Freud described a mental process in which remembered experience is transformed creatively by the imagination into dreams. There are many possible points at which Nabokov's triumph of artistic recollection meets Freud's victory of creative remembrance.

In *The Interpretation of Dreams,* Freud relates the background for a particular dream as follows: A father, who had tended to his dying boy for days, loses him. That night the father dreamed that "his child was standing beside his bed, caught him by the arm and whispered to him reproachfully: 'Father, don't you see I'm burning?'" (509). Waking up, the father rushes into the adjoining room to find the watchman asleep and his son's dead body burned by one of the candles that had fallen. The logical explanation of the dream—that the glaring light from the flame caused the dreaming man to arrive in sleep at an appropriate waking solution—does not concern Freud especially. What Freud finds significant is why the father continued to sleep at all. Here is his explanation:

> And here we shall observe that this dream, too, contained the fulfillment of a wish. The dead child behaved in the dream like a living one: he himself warned his father, came to his bed, and caught him by the arm, just as he had probably done on the occasion from the memory of which the first part of the child's words in the dream were derived. For the sake of the fulfillment of this wish the father prolonged his sleep by one moment. The dream was preferred to a waking reflection because it was able to show the child as once more alive. If the father had woken up first and then made the inference that led him to go into the next room, he would, as it were, have shortened his child's life by that moment of time. (510)

Sleep and the creative process of dreaming thus constitute an imaginative act by which mundane life is improved; in

Nabokov's words, "everything is as it should be, nothing will ever change, nobody will ever die" (*Speak, Memory,* 77). The tyrant of death is destroyed momentarily by the continuation of the dream in which the child is no longer dead but rather alive and only in peril of dying. Creative memory (for Nabokov) or imaginative dreaming (for Freud) compensate for the disappointments of an inadequate reality.

At the end of *The Real Life of Sebastian Knight,* the narrator recalls a dream in which his half-brother Sebastian appears: "I heard Sebastian's voice behind me. . . . I knew he was calling me and saying something very important—and promising to tell me something more important still, if only I came to the corner where he sat or lay, trapped by the heavy sacks that had fallen across his legs." Immediately upon awakening, the narrator receives a cable that Sebastian's "state [is] hopeless come immediately" (189–90). Traveling desperately from England to France, he "experienced the hideous feeling that I had just been jerked awake after dozing heavily for an unknown length of time" (199).

He arrives at the hospital and is taken up to his brother's room: Sebastian had suffered a heart attack and was not to be disturbed from his sleep. The narrator sits quietly in the room with his brother. Here are his thoughts:

> My hands still shook, but I felt happy. He was alive. He was peacefully asleep . . . there was hope. . . . His presence in the next room, the faint sound of breathing, gave me a sense of security, of peace, of wonderful relaxation . . . as soon as he could listen to me, I should

44

tell him that whether he liked it or not I would never be far from him any more. . . . That gentle breathing was telling me more of Sebastian than I had ever known before. If I could have smoked, my happiness would have been perfect. (202–3)

But after some time he is informed by a nurse that a mistake has been made: Sebastian Knight "died yesterday, and you've been visiting Monsieur Kegan" (204). Nevertheless, the narrator insists on the integrity of his misperception since it, like Freud's description of the father's dream that his dead son was yet alive, fulfilled the wish that life be preserved: "Those few minutes I spent listening to what I thought was his breathing changed my life as completely as it would have been changed, had Sebastian spoken to me before dying" (204).

There is a fertile region in common between Nabokov's belief in a creative compensatory memory process and Freud's theory of imaginative dreams preserving the events of the remembered past. By thinking that Monsieur Kegan was his half-brother Sebastian, the narrator asserts that it was as if Kegan were Sebastian: his life was changed "as completely as it would have been changed" in either case. But late in his career, in 1937 (only three years before Nabokov published *Sebastian Knight*), Freud came to believe that constructions in analysis may achieve the equivalent of truth:

The path that starts from the analyst's construction ought to end in the patient's recollection; but it does not always lead so far. Quite often we do not succeed in bringing the patient to recollect what has been re-pressed. Instead of that, if the analysis is carried out correctly, we produce in him an assured conviction of the truth of the construction which achieves the same therapeutic result as a recaptured memory." ("Constructions in Analysis," 265–66)

Whether we remember or create, life is changed "as com-pletely as it would have been changed." What matters, then, is the imaginative process by which we remember—or con-struct—the narrative of what we take to be our lives. Mem-ory equals dream: they meet on the field of art. For both writers, then: "Memory is, really, in itself, a tool, one of the many tools that an artist uses" (Nabokov, *Strong Opinions*, 12). "The work of analysis involves an *art* of interpretation" (Freud, *An Autobiographical Study*, 41).

*H*ere, There, and Everywhere

A small boy of one-and-a-half is engaged in a game of his own invention. While his grandfather observes, he plays with a length of string attached to a wooden spool. He throws the spool over the edge of his cot so that it may not be seen; while doing this, he utters "o-o-o-o." His grandfather and the boy's mother suppose that this sound was an attempt by the boy to say the German word "*fort*" ("gone"). The boy then pulls on the string and makes the spool reappear while uttering "*da*" (German for "there"). In a variation on this game, the boy makes himself disappear: first, he sees his reflection in a full-length mirror; then, by bending over, he is able to remove his reflection and be "gone." The grandfather who watches the boy at play is Sigmund Freud. The boy is Ernst, his daughter Sophie's child. And the game the boy pursues is a game of "disappearance and return . . . [where] the greater pleasure was attached to the second act" (*Beyond the Pleasure Principle,* 15).

Although the game is of disappearance and return, much of the time the boy makes things (toys, objects) disappear as a game-in-itself. By witnessing the complete game, Freud was able to interpret what had been perplexing behavior on the part of his grandson. Freud speculates that the game is the boy's means of coming to terms with his mother's occasional absences. The boy reenacts—with objects that are entirely within his control—a drama of presence and absence that had been beyond his control. The frustration at the loss of the mother's constant attention is compensated by the newly attained sense of mastery: I may not be able to make Mother appear when she is gone, but I am able to bring back this wooden spool, or this toy, etc. Thus, the things that happen *to* the boy are alleviated to an extent by the things he is able to *make* happen.

Freud views the boy's achievement in the game as the conversion of a powerless role to a powerful one: "At the onset he was in a *passive* situation—he was overpowered by the experience; but, by repeating it, unpleasurable though it was, as a game, he took on an *active* part. These efforts might be put down to an instinct for mastery that was acting independently of whether the memory was in itself pleasurable or not" (*Beyond the Pleasure Principle,* 16). As a result of a game, the experiences of life (which one endures passively) are recast as active mastery, as control. By repeating the unpleasurable experience in different form—as a game—one gains mastery and is no longer "overpowered by the experience." In a similar fashion, Nabokov devoted himself to fictional creation, a pursuit that he always described in terms of the game of chess. For instance, "deception in chess, as in art, is only part of the game" and chess problems "demand from the composer the same virtues that characterize all worthwhile art" (*Strong Opinions,* 11, 160–61).

The game, according to Freud, allowed one "to express similar hostile impulses by throwing away objects instead of persons"; it would be possible, as a result, "to work over in the mind some overpowering experience so as to make oneself master of it" (*Beyond the Pleasure Principle,* 16). To throw away a person in life would be cruel; but to throw away a character—an object, really—in a fiction, in the "game of art," establishes mastery. What was Nabokov's attitude in this regard? "I work hard, I work long, on a body of words until it grants me complete possession and pleasure" (*Strong Opinions,* 115). He who possesses a body of words is its master. What was Nabokov's relation to his characters? "My characters are galley slaves" (*Strong Opinions,* 95).

The game of disappearance and return is so satisfying because it mimics and overcomes—within a controlled field—the threat of death. In "Psychopathic Characters on the Stage," Freud noted that drama (and, we may suppose, all literary art) "appeases, as it were, a rising rebellion against the divine regulation of the universe, which is responsible for the existence of suffering" (306). Nabokov's "game of art" likewise expressed his own need to "fight the utter degradation, ridicule, and horror of having developed an infinity of sensation and thought within a finite existence" (*Speak, Memory*, 297). Artistic mastery fulfills to a limited degree what is "innermost in man . . . the spiritual pleasure derivable from the possibilities of outtugging and outrunning gravity, of overcoming or reenacting the earth's pull" (*Speak, Memory*, 301).

Jacques Derrida, who first highlighted the metaphorical potential of the "gone/there" game as detailed by Freud in *Beyond the Pleasure Principle,* describes the possibilities of the gamesman-artist with great perceptiveness: "He makes himself disappear, he masters himself symbolically, he plays with death as if with himself, and he makes himself reappear henceforth without a mirror, in his disappearance itself, maintaining himself like his mother on the line" ("To Speculate—On 'Freud,'" 247). Nabokov's novels demonstrate how acutely Derrida's observation applies as a statement of artistic process. Fictional characters are objects, things, creations—distanced from the author and under his masterful control. According to Freud, any discomfort that might ensue from the real-life situations that are elaborately reworked within the art is "mitigated by the certainty that, firstly, it is someone other than himself who is acting and suffering on the stage, and secondly, that after all it is only a game, which can threaten no damage to his personal security" ("Psycho-pathic Characters on the Stage," 306).

But there is another dimension to the "gone/there" game. The game enabled Freud's grandson, Ernst, to master the temporary absences of his mother. The world, however, conspired against this aesthetic mastery by securing the permanent absence of the boy's mother: while Freud was writing *Beyond the Pleasure Principle,* his daughter Sophie, Ernst's mother, died unexpectedly. There would be no return to follow this disappearance. In a restrained footnote to the text, Freud wrote: "When this child was five and three-quarters, his mother died. Now that she was really 'gone' ('o-o-o'), the little boy showed no signs of grief" (*Beyond the Pleasure Principle,* 16). Was little Ernst without grief because the game had provided a means of detachment? Had the game enabled the boy to gain mastery over the inequities of life? We may suppose, however, that Freud imagined Ernst's response to be like his own; in a letter written shortly after Sophie's death, he mused, "I do as much work as I can, and am grateful for the distraction . . . as for mourning, that will no doubt come later" (Max Schur, *Freud: Living and Dying,* 330). At this unhappy time, writing was Freud's game of art by which a fragile mastery might be attained. The anonymity with which he describes his grandson, the ironic expression "really 'gone'" (as opposed to the temporary "gone" of Sophie's limited absences during her life), the poignant repetition (minus one "o") of the little boy's expression, "o-o-o" (so inadequate in the face of the enormity of his mother's permanent absence, death)—all of this reflects how Freud's use of the incident was a means for him "to work over in the mind some overpowering experience so as to make oneself master of it."

For Nabokov, who experienced the loss of his homeland, language, father, and brother, mastery is attained through the game of art by "diminishing large things and enlarging small ones" (*Speak, Memory,* 167). The crucial "absences" of home and family are overcome in *Speak, Memory* by the linguistic mastery of the evocation of a lost world: "I see again. . . . Everything is as it should be, nothing will ever change, nobody will ever die" (77). The actual losses are mentioned in tight-lipped, mournful brevity.

But Nabokov details in *Speak, Memory* his own version of the game of disappearance and return in which he too made himself disappear and reappear: by enlisting an adult to move a divan away from the wall, four-year-old Vladimir had

> the fantastic pleasure of creeping through that pitch-dark tunnel, where I lingered a little to listen to the singing in my ears—that lonesome vibration so familiar to small boys in dusty hiding places—and then, in a

burst of delicious panic, on rapidly thudding hands and knees I would reach the tunnel's far end, push its cushion away, and be welcomed by a mesh of sunshine on the parquet under the canework of a Viennese chair and two gamesome flies settling by turns. (23)

Nabokov's drama of presence and absence is played by himself: that portion of the self that disappears and the portion that witnesses its reappearance. Thus, as Derrida noted about young Ernst, the self is mastered symbolically. Of course, in writing this scene, Nabokov insisted that it was a game of "the primordial cave" and "not what Freudian mystics might suppose" (22).

In his fiction, moreover, we find the correlative to little Ernst's mirror variation of the "gone/there" game: the notion that the artistic rendition of our recollections can replace—at least to a certain extent—the people and things we have lost. Writing provides a reciprocity of configuration between those departed and the surviving writer. Sineusov, the grieving widower in "Ultima Thule," directly addresses through writing his dead wife: "If you don't remember, then I remember for you: the memory of you can pass, grammatically speaking at least, for your memory, and I am perfectly willing to grant for the sake of an ornate phrase that if, after your death, I and the world still endure, it is only because you recollect the world and me" (*A Russian Beauty*, 149).

For both Freud and Nabokov, writing is a crucial game of

disappearance and return that diminishes the large thing of death and enlarges the small thing of words: death becomes unreal, a thing mastered, and those dead are here, there, and everywhere. . . .

*K*rug and Mourning: The Simple Reality of Things

"All novelists of any worth are psychological novelists," Nabokov declared (*Strong Opinions,* 174). But of course, he was referring to a psychological insight that would be uncontaminated by Freud or psychoanalysis. Freud, however, maintained that "the creative writer cannot evade the psychiatrist nor the psychiatrist the creative writer, and the poetic treatment of a psychiatric theme can turn out to be correct without any sacrifice of its beauty" ("Delusions and Dreams in Jensen's *Gradiva,*" 44). In other words, a novel may have meaning psychoanalytically without a depreciation of its ability to have meaning artistically. For this reason, Freud was untroubled when Wilhelm Jensen, the author of *Gradiva* (a work in which both Freud and Jung were interested), had disavowed any psychological connection to his work. "The author need have known nothing of these [psychoanalytic] rules and purposes, so that he could disavow them in good faith, but that nevertheless we have not discovered anything in his work that is not already in it" ("Jensen's *Gradiva,* 91–92).

It is to be expected, therefore, that a work by a psychological novelist such as Nabokov would have "already in it" powerful insights about the mental processes. Such is the case with *Bend Sinister*. Although he disavowed (in his foreword to the novel) any connection to the "literature of social comment" (*Bend Sinister*, vi), he also (in a 1969 interview) described it as an "absolutely final indictment of Russian and German totalitarianism" (*Strong Opinions*, 156). When he insisted that *Bend Sinister* "is not really about life and death in a grotesque police state" while also admitting that he had included "bits of Lenin's speeches . . . a chunk of the Soviet constitution, and gobs of Nazist pseudo-efficiency" (*Bend Sinister*, vii), he was asserting that tyrants are not real, are fictional, ought not to exist, and thus do not exist within the author's world as anything but fiction. Recall the conclusion of the narrator in his story "Tyrants Destroyed": "Laughter, actually, saved me . . . in my efforts to make him terrifying, I have only made him ridiculous, thereby destroying him—an old, proven method" (*Tyrants Destroyed*, 36). Thus, the oppressive regime of *Bend Sinister* (as Nabokov would wish for all such regimes) is seen at the end of the novel to be "harmlessly fading away when I dismiss the cast" (*Bend Sinister*, viii).

In any psychological drama, Freud suggested, "The struggle that causes the suffering is fought out in the hero's mind itself—a struggle between different impulses, and one which must have its end in the extinction, not of the hero, but of one of his impulses; it must end, that is to say, in a renunciation" ("Psychopathic Characters on the Stage," 308). In Nabokov's *Bend Sinister,* Adam Krug experiences just such a "struggle between different impulses," and the novel ends with just such a renunciation. Freud had described mourning as "the reaction to the loss of a loved person, or to the loss of some abstraction which has taken the place of one, such as one's country, liberty, an ideal, and so on" ("Mourning and Melancholia," 243). Nabokov acutely represents both losses as contributing to Krug's sorrow: he mourns for his deceased wife, his country, his liberty, and ultimately, his son and his conscience. Nabokov enunciated the "main theme" of *Bend Sinister* as "the beating of Krug's loving heart, the torture an intense tenderness is subjected to." But he also proposed "two other themes": "dim-brained brutality," and "Krug's blessed madness when he suddenly perceives the simple reality of things and knows but cannot express in the words of his world that he and his son and his wife and everybody else are merely my whims and megrims" (viii).

Krug is a man in mourning, and, in Freud's words, "in mourning it is the world which has become poor and empty" ("Mourning and Melancholia," 246). But Krug's world is bleak not merely because of the loss of his wife but also because his country has been taken over by an absurd dictator who was once his ridiculous schoolmate, Paduk. Krug is unable to substitute love of country or liberty for the love of his dead wife, for all of them have already been seized from him. There remain only his son and his integrity, and it is Paduk's heinous cruelty to coerce Krug's endorsement of his regime by kidnaping the man's son; thus, Krug is indeed faced with a struggle between impulses—and whatever his choice, mourning remains his fate.

Mourning is a task, a process in which "time is needed for the command of reality-testing to be carried out in detail, and . . . when this work has been accomplished the ego will have succeeded in freeing its libido from the lost object" ("Mourning and Melancholia," 252). But if reality-testing reveals a world so bleak and horrific that it is more rewarding to dwell upon the lost object, then the work of mourning may not proceed. Why should Krug free his libido from the loving memories of his wife when a world of cruelty and barbarism awaits him? Mourning also includes the guilt of the mourner for surviving, which must also be worked through: "The ego, confronted as it were with the question whether it shall share this fate [of death], is persuaded by the sum of the narcissistic satisfactions it derives from being alive to sever its attachment to the object that has been abolished" ("Mourning and Melancholia," 255). But when the world provides insufficient narcissistic satisfactions, there is no reason to sever the attachment to the lost object. For Krug, Paduk's power seems less real than the imagined reality of Krug's departed wife.

Krug decides to endorse the dictatorship in exchange for his son's freedom only to discover that his son has been savagely murdered by "accident." The regime, incredibly, holds Krug to his end of the bargain: "We cannot believe that any personal bereavement can come between you and our Ruler" (*Bend Sinister*, 228). When Krug, his world destroyed, refuses to cooperate, he is imprisoned. And there, the struggle between the regime and Krug reaches an impasse. In a wretched world that provides no gratification, there can be no relinquishment of the lost object: there can be no release from mourning. Freud, referring to a similar psychoanalytic impasse, noted that "an association often comes to a stop precisely before the genuine dream-thought: it has only had contact with it through allusions. At that point we intervene on our own; we fill in the hints, draw undeniable conclusions, and give explicit utterance to what the patient has only touched on in his associations" (*New Introductory Lectures,* 12).

Nabokov, the author-as-analyst, intervenes in the fiction in an analogous way: "Just before his reality, his remembered hideous misfortune could pounce upon him—it was then that I felt a pang of pity for Adam and slid towards him along an inclined beam of pale light—causing instantaneous madness, but at least saving him from the senseless agony of his logical fate" (*Bend Sinister,* 233). Nabokov draws the "undeniable conclusion" that madness is the only alternative to Krug's "logical fate"—the "senseless agony" of perpetual mourning. But again the world impinges. Before the firing squad, Krug madly believes that he and Paduk are again youngsters playing in the school playground. The widower charges his old playmate, the dictator, as the prison guards fire. It is at this point—when it would seem that nothing could be done to save Krug—that Nabokov again intervenes: "And just a fraction of an instant before another and better bullet hit him, he shouted again: You, you—and the wall vanished, like a rapidly withdrawn slide, and I stretched myself and got up from among the chaos of written and rewritten pages, to investigate the sudden twang that something had made in striking the wire netting of my window" (*Bend Sinister,* 240).

By transforming Krug into a moth, Nabokov transforms the novelistic scene into the scene of writing: he thus achieves a renunciation of the world—that world, the oppressive world, the mourner's world "which has become poor and empty," but which now stands revealed as a mirage, a fiction. Nabokov's intervention enables Krug to perceive "a rent in his world leading to another world of tenderness, brightness and beauty" (*Bend Sinister,* ix)—the world of the author, the world of art, the world, in Freud's phrase, of "narcissistic satisfactions [that] derive from being alive."

"The simple reality of things" for Krug results in a "blessed madness" that relieves him from his mourning and his death: he achieves an immortality of sorts as a fictional character within a novel by Nabokov, an author creating during "a particularly cloudless and vigorous period of life" (*Bend Sinister,* viii, v). And why shouldn't it be, for when the "poor and empty" desolation of World War II has receded, reality-testing again reveals a satisfying picture, and the "narcissistic satisfactions" of literary creation can relegate mourning to the text, rendering death as nothing "but a question of style" (*Bend Sinister,* 241).

*I*n My Private Sky

The first interview included in *Strong Opinions* was given in New York in 1962; Nabokov had traveled there for the opening of the film *Lolita*. In response to a question about writing the screenplay of *Lolita,* Nabokov described how he had refused the initial offer to write the script but had then been urged to reconsider. "The hardest part was taking the plunge—deciding to undertake the task. . . . I traveled once more to Hollywood and there, under the jacarandas, worked for six months on the thing. . . . I knew that if I did not write the script somebody else would, and I also knew that at best the end product in such cases is less of a blend than a collision of interpretations" (6). About the director Stanley Kubrick, he "derived the impression that he was an artist" and thus eagerly awaited "seeing a plausible *Lolita*" at the opening (7).

Two years later, in 1964, Nabokov was asked his opinion of the film of which "you finally wrote the screenplay yourself." Nabokov "thought the movie was absolutely first-rate." Noting that he "had nothing to do with the actual production," he remarked: "All I did was write the screenplay, a preponderating portion of which was used by Kubrick." Nabokov's only reservation was that he might have stressed "certain things that were not stressed—for example, the different motels at which they stayed"; but on the whole, he referred to the "moments of unforgettable acting and directing" (*Strong Opinions,* 21).

After an interval of two years, in 1966, Nabokov, in an interview, commented on a new project: "a huge screenplay based on *Lolita*. I wrote it for Kubrick who used only bits and shadows of it for his otherwise excellent film" (*Strong Opinions,* 90). Thus, what had been a "preponderating portion" of his work had now become "only bits and shadows" of his contributed screenplay.

A second interview given during the same period also prompted the announcement of

> another project I have been nursing for some time . . . the publication of the complete screenplay of *Lolita* that I made for Kubrick. Although there are just enough borrowings from it in his version to justify my legal position as author of the script, the film is only a blurred skimpy glimpse of the marvelous picture I imagined and set down scene by scene during the six months I worked in a Los Angeles villa. I do not wish to imply that Kubrick's film is mediocre; in its own right, it is first-rate, but it is not what I wrote. . . . I shall never understand why he did not follow my directions and dreams. It is a great pity. (*Strong Opinions,* 105–6)

In four years, then, as described in the interviews Nabokov so carefully included in his collection of public statements, he was transformed from the solitary author of the script ("If I did not write the script somebody else would") to the dominant contributor who wrote the "preponderating portion" of the text used in the film, to a concealed, ghostly presence in the "bits and shadows" of his work incorporated within the film, to a disappointed author-in-name-only who sees the film as a mere "blurred skimpy glimpse" of his own creation: "It is not what I wrote."

What happened to account for this change? I find it impossible to believe that Nabokov would consciously misrepresent his share of the contribution in order to attract a larger readership for his published screenplay. Every statement was issued in complete sincerity. We know how much a conscious process the construction of an interview was for Nabokov. What has occurred is a dramatic alteration of the way Nabokov thought about his screenplay. It matters little whether Nabokov was correct to assert that the film was preponderatingly his, or whether he was correct to state that it was not what he wrote; what matters is that he held both of these opinions within a four-year period.

The actual six-month period during which he wrote his screenplay for *Lolita* had become a memory. In order to gain a sense of how this memory evolved for Nabokov, it is worth considering his attitude about memories. He was once asked whether, in his "acute scrutiny of the past," he could "find the instruments that fashioned" him. His answer was "yes—unless I refashion them retrospectively, by the very act of evoking them" (*Strong Opinions*, 142). He was not bothered, he remarked, by distortion of recollected detail: "The distortion of a remembered image may not only enhance its beauty with an added refraction, but provide informative links with earlier or later patches of the past" (*Strong Opinions,* 143). Thus the telling becomes inseparable from the tale. Memories are changed by summoning them, by forming them into verbal representations, but these modifications, far from disturbing the "truth," serve to "enhance its beauty with an added refraction." Nabokov cheerfully admitted that "even the most talented and conscientious historian may err. In other words, I do not believe that 'history' exists apart from the historian" (*Strong Opinions,* 138).

An artist "refashions [his memories] retrospectively, by the very act of evoking them." Past events become a part of the narrative enterprise of ordering them—the past becomes the time of the telling, the time of the present. "An artist invents his own world," Nabokov remarked, " . . . how can he be said to influence his own understanding of what he has created himself?" (*Strong Opinions,* 136). The history of a Nabokov memory informs us about the historian who recounts it. The past and its memories are not *back there,* in time, but *in here,* within the mind, able to be evoked and molded like the materials of fictional creation.

In his sensitive essay, "Narration in the Psychoanalytic Dialogue," Roy Schafer proposed that there is

a narrative form that is methodologically more adequate to the psychoanalytic occasion [than the psychoanalytic life history]. . . . It is a story that begins in the middle, which is the present: the beginning is the beginning of the analysis. . . . Once the analysis is under way . . . more and more [the present] seems to be both a repetitive, crisis-perpetuating misremembering of the past and a way of living defensively with respect to a future which is, in the most disruptive way, imagined fearfully and irrationally on the model of the past. (52)

We misremember in order to maintain a story about ourselves that is more gratifying, in some way, than the story that proceeds from the past; at the same time, our attitude toward the future is influenced strongly by precisely that portion of the past that we have modified through misremembering.

Freud, in *The Ego and the Id,* remarked that the ego fears an "external danger," and "the fear is of being overwhelmed or annihilated" (57). The writing of a screenplay would, in this sense, appear as a more fearful enterprise than the solitary composition of a novel: once the text is completed, the film goes into production—then the writer who is the author of the script becomes secondary to the *auteur* who is the director of the film. It is not difficult to perceive how—to a writer who maintained the importance of singleminded composition—the prospect of a collaboration (no matter how convivial) between writer and director might be regarded as an external danger. "I shall never understand why he did not follow my directions": I am in charge, I call the shots; all you need to do is "set down scene by scene the marvelous picture I imagined." When this is not possible, there is the fear of the writer's ego, his creative self, being overwhelmed or annihilated.

The creative changes that Nabokov crafted in his account of the *Lolita* screenplay are characteristic of the fictional energies with which Nabokov approached the creation of a public personality: he cherished "the opportunity . . . to construct in the presence of my audience the semblance of what I hope is a plausible and not altogether displeasing personality" (*Strong Opinions,* 158). Plausible and not displeasing for whom? The answer may be found in Nabokov's belief that "the felicity of a phrase is shared by writer and reader: by the satisfied writer and the grateful reader" (*Strong Opinions,* 40). The audience "witnesses" the illusion of the construction of a personality—one that is plausible and not displeasing to its creator. From this, he is satisfied and the reader is meant to be grateful.

And part of that construction is the formulation of a story about the writer: one that characteristically misremembers to avoid an external danger—in this case, authorial collaboration. Again and again, Nabokov insisted that he was alone, unto himself, unique: "No creed or school has had any influence on me whatsoever." "I do not believe that any particular writer has had any definite influence upon me." "I've never been influenced by anyone in particular, dead or quick. . . . I'm the shuttlecock above the Atlantic, and how bright and blue it is there, in my private sky" (*Strong Opinions,* 3, 46, 116–17).

*O*n the Borderline

In *Beyond the Pleasure Principle,* Freud wrote of consciousness and the perceptual systems that they "must lie on the borderline between outside and inside; [they] must be turned towards the external world and must envelop the other psychical systems" (24). The ego's role of mediation between the internal and external worlds is simultaneously a burden of differentiation: what constitutes inside? what constitutes outside? how may I tell the difference? Similarly, Freud addressed the polarity between the ego and the external world as a conflict of "the real" in "Instincts and Their Vicissitudes" (140). The ego's ability to distinguish between inside and outside is assisted by reality-testing, the process of assessing one's inner sense of the real with one's outer sense of it—not unlike the comparison of an interpretation to the text. But there is no text about which interpreters are unanimously in agreement; nor is the world a fixed point from which reliable measurements may proceed. Thus, when we dwell on the borderline between outside and inside, we are faced with a process that is analogous to the comparison of two divergent interpretations—without a text as a point of reference.

The narrator in Nabokov's "'That in Aleppo Once . . .'" writes to the author (a fictional version of Nabokov, named "V.") that he has arrived in New York from war-torn Europe: "Although I can produce documentary proofs of matrimony, I am positive now that my wife never existed. You may know her name from some other source, but that does not matter: it is the name of an illusion. Therefore, I am able to speak of her with as much detachment as I would of a character in a story (one of your stories, to be precise)" (*Nabokov's Dozen,* 142). One reason for the narrator's detachment is that he and his wife *are* characters in a story: the letter is the story, and the narrator's fate will be determined by the author. The narrator feels as if he had been married; he has a marriage license as evidence, but external events have provided contradictory evidence to negate his certainty. In effect, the narrator is describing a conflict of opposing drives (or "instincts" in the English *Standard Edition* of Freud) that derives from the "sharp distinction between ego-instincts which we equated with death instincts, and sexual instincts, which we equated with life instincts" (*Beyond the Pleasure Principle,* 52–53).

The narrator marries (affirms life) in the midst of a time of death; a few weeks later, the Nazis occupy Paris. The newlyweds flee Paris because the narrator (also an author) had earlier criticized the Nazi regime. But as they travel, he realizes that they do not fear Hitler, "a booted and buckled fool," but rather "something of which he was a mere symbol, something monstrous and impalpable, a timeless and faceless mass of immemorial horror" (*Nabokov's Dozen,* 144). The couple is on a journey that confirms, in Freud's words, "the struggle between Eros and Death, between the instinct of life and the instinct of destruction, as it works itself out in the human species. This struggle is what all life essentially consists of" (*Civilization and Its Discontents,* 122).

During their train trip to Nice, the narrator and his wife

are separated accidentally. Throughout the week they are apart, the narrator searches for her but when he hears "those . . . who chanced to have Jewish blood talk of their doomed kinsmen crammed into hell-bound trains," his "own plight, by contrast, acquired a commonplace air of irreality" (*Nabokov's Dozen,* 146). Reality-testing will not help the narrator, for the world's plight is more severe and desperate than his own. As a result of comparing his inner world to the outer world, the narrator acquires a sense of "irreality." This feeling only intensifies when his wife, upon her return, tells him initially a "hazy but banal" account of misguided wanderings and then changes her story: she had spent the time with a man from the train. The narrator becomes obsessed with determining every detail of his wife's indiscretion: "But the limit of desired knowledge was unattainable, nor could I ever foretell the approximate point after which I might imagine myself satiated, because of course the denominator of every fraction of knowledge was potentially as infinite as the number of intervals between the fractions themselves" (*Nabokov's Dozen,* 148).

Throughout this emotional ordeal, the narrator is struggling to obtain passports for their emigration to the United States. Distraught, he "sank down on a stone bench weeping and cursing a mock world where millions of lives were being juggled by the clammy hands of consuls and *commissaires*" (149). The turbulence of inside is matched by the chaos of outside: as a result, the world is artificial. Like his wife, it is an illusion, it never existed.

When his wife confesses that she had *not,* after all, slept with the man from the train, the narrator perceives his wife "glimmer and fade"; although he accepts her story, "the happier our new relations seemed, the stronger I felt an undercurrent of poignant sadness" (149–50). On the eve of their departure, the wife disappears with all her belongings. He hears from their angry friends a litany of his supposed offenses; his wife, for instance, was in love with a wealthy Frenchman but the narrator had refused to grant a divorce. The conversation culminates with his "ultimate misdeed": "I shall never forgive you," an old woman tells him, "her dog, that poor beast which you hanged with your own hands before leaving Paris" (151). All of this is utter fiction to the narrator: is his wife crazy? is he crazy? is the world crazy? Distinctions between inside and outside are impossible, as the violence, senselessness, and instability of the world-at-war are mirrored in the stories concocted by his wife. Concluding that "she had gone, that was the end," the narrator sails for New York alone.

On the ship, he hears that his wife had been waiting for him on the embankment in Marseilles: "She said that I would presently join her with bag and tickets" (152). Is this another of his wife's insane reversals? The fact remains that she is stranded in wartime France without funds or provisions. The narrator concludes: "I suddenly knew for certain that she had never existed at all" (152). Freud, in *Beyond the Pleasure Principle,* remarked that "a particular way is adopted of dealing with any internal excitations which produce too great an increase of unpleasure: there is a tendency to treat them as though they were acting, not from the inside, but from the outside" (29). The origin of any drive, Freud noted, is traced "to a need to restore an earlier state of things" (57). Accordingly, the narrator insists that "life had been real before, life will be real from now on, I hope. Not tomorrow, though. Perhaps after tomorrow" (152–53).

The narrator is haunted by the feeling that he has somehow caused this calamity. Thoughts of his wife wandering in Marseilles torment him: "She keeps on walking to and fro where the brown nets are spread to dry on the hot stone slabs and the dappled light of the water plays on the side of a moored fishing boat. Somewhere, somehow, I have made some fatal mistake" (153). According to Freud, "What psycho-analysis reveals in the transference phenomena of neurotics can also be observed in the lives of some normal people. The impression they give is of being pursued by a malignant fate or possessed by some 'daemonic' power; but psycho-analysis has always taken the view that their fate is for the most part arranged by themselves" (*Beyond the Pleasure Principle*, 21). What is crucial is that the outside merges with the inside. In his "Introduction to *Psychoanalysis and the War Neuroses*," Freud proposed that, as a result of war, "the human ego is defending itself from a danger which threatens it from without or which is embodied in a shape assumed by the ego itself. . . . What is feared is nevertheless an internal enemy" (210).

In his misery and guilt, the narrator imagines himself as a modern Othello: "It may end in *Aleppo* if I am not careful.

Spare me, V.: you would load your dice with an unbearable implication if you took that for a title" (153). Since that is the story's title, we may assume that the narrator will follow Othello's lead and commit suicide out of remorse at his responsibility for his wife's fate. But was he responsible? In *Civilization and Its Discontents,* Freud maintained that "we can only suspect [a death drive] as something in the background behind Eros, and it escapes detection unless its presence is betrayed by its being alloyed with Eros" (121). On the borderline of inside and outside, at a time of death and destruction, the ambivalent narrator's love is commingled with death. What actually happened, what he had intended to happen, what will happen—all are as confused as his sense of "the real." He appeals to V., to art, to provide an outside, a fixed point of orientation, a direction that determines his fate. And thus, as a character in V.'s and Nabokov's story, he becomes writing, which, in Jacques Derrida's words, "neither lives nor dies; it lives *on*" ("Border Lines," 103).

*S*plitting of the Ego

Vladimir Nabokov described himself as a "mild old gentleman" who just happened to create "pretty beastly" characters that were "beyond the limits" of his own identity (*Strong Opinions,* 19, 13). His "vague, old-fashioned liberalism," committed to "freedom of speech, freedom of thought, freedom of art," nevertheless accommodated a conception of art as being "fantastically deceitful" (*Strong Opinions,* 113, 34, 33).

He devoted significant energies to describing the regularity of his work habits and routines in his interviews; but when criticized by Edmund Wilson for an "addiction to rare and unfamiliar words," his response was, "It does not occur to him that I may have rare and unfamiliar things to convey" (*Strong Opinions,* 250). His motive for writing his books was "for the sake of the pleasure, for the sake of the difficulty . . . I just like composing riddles with elegant solutions." Yet when he was asked whether his artistic credo might be "all is vanity," he answered: "I believe that one day a reappraiser will come and declare that, far from being a frivolous firebird, I was a rigid moralist kicking sin, cuffing stupidity, ridiculing the vulgar and cruel—and assigning sovereign power to tenderness, talent, and pride" (*Strong Opinions,* 16, 193). His "notions of strategy" for chess problems (and metaphorically, for art) were "deceit, to the point of diabolism, and originality, verging upon the grotesque" (*Speak, Memory,* 289); however, his "existence has always remained . . . harmonious and green" (*Strong Opinions,* 145).

How is it possible for the mild to coexist with the grotesque, for the moralist to create with diabolic deceit? In a perceptive article, Charles Baxter suggested that Nabokov's esthetics might embody a duality: Nabokov's "novels are meant to be considered as self-enclosed imaginative systems that reflect, in a way that cannot be formulated, a condition that escapes mimesis and yet is aesthetically 'true' to itself" ("Nabokov, Idolatry, and the Police State," 815). The important phrase is "in a way that cannot be formulated." Sigmund

Freud, late in his life, addressed himself to precisely this problem, and formulated a way that accounts for "two attitudes persist[ing] side by side throughout their lives without influencing each other" (*An Outline of Psycho–Analysis*, 203).

Freud's "Splitting of the Ego in the Process of Defence" may offer some insight into Nabokov's characteristic division between normality and grotesquerie, compassion and hostility. In certain instances, an idea within the ego may "split off" from that conceptual realm. When this occurs, an individual may maintain two contradictory attitudes simultaneously. "On the one hand," Freud recounted, "with the help of certain mechanisms he rejects reality and refuses to accept any prohibition; on the other hand, in the same breath he recognizes the danger of reality, takes over the fear of that danger as a pathological symptom and tries subsequently to divest himself of the fear. It must be confessed that this is a very ingenious solution of the difficulty" ("Splitting of the Ego in the Process of Defence," 275). To reject reality and in the same breath observe it sufficiently to recognize its danger is not unlike Baxter's observation that Nabokov's novels could escape mimesis and yet be true to themselves. Freud's label of "ingenious" leads to the idea that such defensive maneuvering maintains a creative component.

Whenever a contradiction is perceived between the outside and the inside, between the world and the text, an adjustment must occur. Freud remarked that "the ego often enough finds itself in the position of fending off some demand from the external world which it feels distressing and that this is effected by means of a *disavowal* of the perceptions which bring to knowledge this demand from reality" (*An Outline of Psycho–Analysis,* 203–4). A disavowal of perceptions: certainly that would describe Nabokov's rejection of general ideas in favor of specific details, as exemplified by his statement, "With absolute lucidity I recall landscapes, gestures, intonations, a million sensuous details, but names and numbers topple into oblivion with absurd abandon like little blind men in file from a pier" (*Strong Opinions,* 140). A fictional world remains true to itself when its creator "disavows" or "fends off demands from the external world" that might disturb its inner consistency.

Describing a particular case history, Freud commented:

> [the boy] created a substitute for the penis which he missed in females—that is to say, a fetish. In so doing, it is true that he had disavowed reality, but he had saved his own penis. . . . [But] the boy did not simply contradict his perceptions and hallucinate a penis where there was none to be seen; he effected no more than a displacement of value. . . . This way of dealing with reality . . . almost deserves to be described as artful. ("Splitting of the Ego," 277)

Might we consider Nabokov's writing as an "artful" fending off or holding off of the world in order to "save" or preserve the purity of a created private realm? What we encounter in Nabokov is an artistic sensibility that knows the world and yet is dedicated to the act of holding off through art precisely the reality that is known by the split-off perceptual realm. Nabokov's concept of "outtugging and outrunning gravity" through writing—his intention of "diminishing large things and enlarging small ones" to arrive at an artistic realm that is superior to life—is appropriate for an author who "did not believe in time" (*Speak, Memory*, 301, 167, 139).

Nabokov's devotion to "complexity and splendid insincerity" in art (*Strong Opinions*, 161) is represented by his preference for "fold[ing] my magic carpet, after use, in such a way as to superimpose one part of the pattern upon another. Let visitors trip" (*Speak, Memory*, 139). And yet he also maintained, with the same intensity, that his "purpose is not to be facetiously flashy or grotesquely obscure but to express what I feel and think with the utmost truthfulness and perception" (*Strong Opinions*, 179). In Freud's words, the "two [contradictory] attitudes persist side by side throughout their lives without influencing each other." Nabokov agreed with an interviewer that his "attachment to childhood [was] specially nostalgic and intense." But the stress, he replied, "is not on Russian Revolution. It could have been anything, an earthquake, an illness, an individual departure prompted by a private disaster. The accent is on the abruptness of the change" (*Strong Opinions*, 148). Freud, in "Analysis Terminable and Interminable," commented that "the adult's ego, with its increased strength, continues to defend itself against dangers which no longer exist in reality; indeed, it finds itself compelled to seek out those situations in reality which can serve as an approximate substitute for the original danger, so as to be able to justify, in relation to them, its maintaining its habitual modes of reaction" (238). Might it be said of Nabokov's writing that it creates alternative "situations in reality" that may serve as "approximate substitute[s]" for the "original danger[s]" that were encountered in life?

In his National Book Award speech, Nabokov evoked his devotion to art: "I enjoy, I have always enjoyed stressing the word 'art,' an unpopular intonation nowadays: art not as a profession, not as a summer commune of kindred minds, and not as a demonstration of topical ideas in a drizzle of politics, but Art with a capital A as big as the biggest Arch of Triumph, art careful and carefree, selfless and self-centered, art burning the brow and cooling the brain" (*The Nabokovian:* 16). "Careful and carefree," "selfless and self-centered," fiery and cold—persisting side by side: perhaps Freud's concept of splitting helps highlight the dynamics of Nabokov's brilliant creation of fiction *and* his creative authorship of himself as a public Author. He fashioned himself as an official personality committed to art, while splitting off that private self whose emotions might interfere with the sanctity of his "Art with a capital A." Thus, depending on the particular scene of writing—the novel or the interview—the grotesque or the regular would achieve its alternative moment of ascendance.

Through the disavowal of certain perceptions and the artistic stylization of others, a displacement of value is achieved. For Nabokov, "reality is a very subjective affair. I can only define it as a kind of gradual accumulation of information; and as a specialization" (*Strong Opinions,* 10). But specialization entails an accumulation that is highly selective. For each aspect that is retained, another is discarded or—disavowed? split off? "The distortion of a text is the work of a tendentious censorship . . . [but] the psychical apparatus is intolerant of unpleasure; it has to fend it off at all costs, and if the perception of reality entails unpleasure, that perception—that is, the truth—must be sacrificed." Who made this statement: Nabokov, in *The Real Life of Sebastian Knight*? or Freud in "Analysis Terminable and Interminable" (237)?

*D*oubles

They are all over the place, these doubles. There are Humbert Humbert (whose very name is a doubling) and Quilty; Sebastian Knight and V.; Hermann and Felix; Kinbote and Shade; Lloyd and Floyd (the double monster); and even, in *Look at the Harlequins!,* Vadim Vadimovich N. and his author, Vladimir Vladimirovich Nabokov. In his autobiography, Nabokov describes himself and his brother Sergey (less than a year's difference in age) in a photograph as "looking like the same infant, wigless and wigged" (*Speak, Memory,* 128). Later in the book, when he struggles to evoke his brother, he admits: "That twisted quest for Sebastian Knight . . . is really nothing in comparison to th[is] task" (257). Nevertheless, when asked in an interview to comment on "the *Doppelgänger* motif," Nabokov's answer was: "The *Doppelgänger* subject is a frightful bore" (*Strong Opinions,* 83). Recalling Nabokov's aversion to general ideas, we may conjecture that the general theme of the double was a "frightful bore," but the creation of specific instances of doubling—ah, that's another matter! When the interviewer continued to inquire about doubles, Nabokov responded: "These murky matters have no importance to me as a writer. Philosophically, I am an indivisible monist. Incidentally, your handwriting is very like mine" (85). In the midst of rejecting the *idea* of doubles, Nabokov is engaged in creating a new set—himself and the interviewer—on the basis of their similar handwriting! The same interviewer, Alfred Appel, Jr., was motivated sufficiently by the doubles theme to assert in the preface to his *Annotated Lolita:* "The annotator exists; he is a veteran and a father, a teacher and a taxpayer, and has not been invented by Vladimir Nabokov" (xii).

And yet, there is still another figure lurking behind all these doubles: the figure of Sigmund Freud. His name is cited in preface after preface, interview after interview, mocked and ridiculed until the aversion to Freud becomes itself a thing Nabokovian, a part of the self that is not the self. Freudians are warned to "keep out" of his novels; his nightmares are "utterly lacking any possible Freudian implication or explication"; a portion of every morning is spent "refuting the Viennese quack" by interpreting his dreams "without using one single reference to sexual symbols or mythical complexes"; psychoanalysis "leads to dangerous ethical consequences": the persona of Freud joins Nabokov's own "beastly" fictional characters who are "outside my inner self like the mournful monsters of a cathedral façade—demons placed there merely to show that they have been booted out" (*Strong Opinions,* 145, 29, 47, 116, 19). In a richly insightful chapter on Nabokov and Freud in *The Talking Cure,* Jeffrey Berman hypothesized: "It is as if Freud is the central figure in Nabokov's life, always shadowing the novelist" (213).

As a result of these relentless attacks on Freud, Nabokov achieved a link with Freud: he insured that whenever the name Nabokov was mentioned, it would conjure up the epithet, "he who hated Freud." In "Scenes from the Life of a Double Monster," Floyd, describing himself and Lloyd, concludes: "Each was eminently normal, but together they formed a monster. Indeed, it is strange to think that the presence of a mere band of tissue, a flap of flesh not much longer than a lamb's liver, should be able to transform joy, pride, tenderness, adoration, gratitude to God into horror and despair" (*Nabokov's Dozen,* 167). This "band" was a "tissue" of words, comprising a bond that Nabokov nurtured throughout his life. Freud, in his *Introductory Lectures,* described ambivalence in a way that sheds light on this bond: "The hostile feelings are as much an indication of an emotional tie as the affectionate ones, in the same way as defiance signifies dependence as much as obedience does, though with a 'minus' instead of a 'plus' sign before it" (443).

In opening up a text by Nabokov, whenever we might forget about the existence of Freud, there is Nabokov, reminding us of Freud's presence and thus establishing him as a figure within Nabokov's world. It is as if Nabokov had a need to create Freud, a fictional Freud who became for Nabokov a manufactured foil or double to his own authorial persona, analogous to those doubles so prevalent in his fiction. The effect is eerie and disconcerting. Freud, in "The 'Uncanny,'" explored this sense: "An uncanny effect is often and easily produced when the distinction between imagination and reality is effaced, as when something that we have hitherto regarded as imaginary appears before us in reality, or when a symbol takes over the full functions of the thing it symbolizes, and so on" (244). Recalling that for Nabokov the creation of a fictional world took precedence over the affairs of the real world, the insertion (by Nabokov) of Freud into his created textual world achieves an "efface[ment] of the distinction between imagination and reality." To ban Freud so vociferously is to give him substance, thing-ness, within Nabokov's world of textual things.

With most of his enunciated strong opinions, Nabokov displayed a sense of discrimination. He was able, for instance, to distinguish and particularize concerning his political beliefs, avoiding a blanket embrace or repudiation of American policy: "In home politics I am strongly anti-segregationist. In foreign policy, I am definitely on the government's side" (*Strong Opinions,* 98). It is instructive to wonder about his inability to express himself in this manner regarding Freud. Could it be that the "symbol [took] over the full functions of the thing it symbolize[d]"?

Otto Rank, in his psychoanalytic study, *The Double,* proposed that "fear and hate with respect to the double-self are closely connected with the narcissistic love for it and with the resistance of this love" (73). Certainly, Nabokov might be said to have borne a "narcissistic love" for his hated fictional creation, "Freud," not unlike his ambivalent attitude toward many of his characters—for instance, Humbert and Van

Veen. Nabokov came to resent those fictional characters upon whom he had bestowed a personal detail, leading him to conclude: "The man in me revolts against the fictionist" (*Speak, Memory,* 95). Nabokov "balked" at the effort of including Sergey in the first version of his memoirs. That brother who "was indifferent to most of the things I was fond of" (257) was refused admittance initially to the cherished written world, and it is no surprise that Rank believed "the double is often identified with the brother" (75).

Freud was no stranger to the ambivalent conflicts engendered by doubles. His relations with such figures as Fliess, Adler, Jung, and Rank bear testament to his experience. In his *Interpretation of Dreams,* he confessed: "My emotional life has always insisted that I should have an intimate friend and a hated enemy. I have always been able to provide myself afresh with both, and it has not infrequently happened that the ideal situation of childhood has been so completely reproduced that friend and enemy have come together in a single individual" (483). It is clear to me that Nabokov had similar needs—Edmund Wilson providing the most conspicuous example. But where Freud "provide[d him]self afresh with both" from life, Nabokov, whenever it was necessary, created his in his fiction. In creating this written depiction of Freud, this fictional double who was "friend and enemy . . . come together in a single individual," Nabokov was tacitly acknowledging the truth of Freud's assertion that "there are many more means of creating uncanny effects in fiction than there are in real life" ("The 'Uncanny,'" 249).

But what about the symbolic dimensions of this propensity for doubles? Freud suggested that "the 'double' was originally an insurance against the destruction of the ego, an 'energetic denial of the power of death,' as Rank says. . . . This invention of doubling as a preservation against extinction has its counterpart in the language of dreams. . . . From having been an assurance of immortality, it becomes the uncanny harbinger of death" ("The 'Uncanny,'" 235). Nabokov's invention of Freud as a foil within his body of writing attests to his desire for life: even as one hates, one lives, and the creation by an author of even a hated character is yet a piece of oneself. But the double who initially bolsters the self remains on the page, "banded" to the author by a "tissue" of words that, in their fixed immobility, are "harbinger[s] of death." The reverse side of the ambivalence is revealed: Nabokov, without his hatred of Freud, is not Nabokov. Without that which is not-me, I am not myself. Nabokov wrote of his brother that "I would creep up behind and prod him in the ribs" (*Speak, Memory,* 257). That "situation of childhood" lives on, artfully "reproduced" in the character of Nabokov's enduring creation, "Sigmund Freud."

*I*nsomnia and Consciousness

Nabokov maintained a lifelong struggle with insomnia. During interviews he provided detailed accounts of his sleeping habits —when he would retire, when he would actually fall asleep, how many times per week he would have nightmares, etc. In a 1975 interview, he made up a story about jogging daily for hours in order to show "how desperate I am beginning to be in my fight with insomnia" ("Checking In with Vladimir Nabokov," 69). Insomnia became, for Nabokov, a metaphor for his artistic consciousness.

In a memorable passage from *Speak, Memory,* Nabokov admitted: "All my life I have been a poor go-to-sleeper." People who fall "immediately" to sleep in trains, and begin snoring "with an offensive familiarity of demeanor . . . amaze me as much as the uninhibited chap who cozily defecates in the presence of a chatty tubber." Why is there this peculiar comparison between sleep and defecation? "Sleep," Nabokov pronounced, "is the most moronic fraternity in the world, with the heaviest dues and the crudest rituals. It is a mental torture I find debasing." Occasionally, he admitted, he would resort to "a strong pill" that provided "an hour or two of frightful nightmares," or else he would nap in the afternoon for "the comic relief," but these measures were "force[d]" upon him by "the strain and drain of composition" (108). The burdens of "Art with a Capital A" weaken the artist and impel him to compromise himself momentarily by resorting to sleep—but only for a few instants, and he certainly did not enjoy himself!

Sleep, Nabokov admitted, was a "nightly betrayal of reason, humanity, genius" that he "simply [could] not get used to." In order for sleep to "betray" reason and humanity, it is necessary for reason, humanity, and genius to be waking functions: not something that exists implicitly, but something that exists-through-action. One is only a genius to the extent that one produces works of genius. Reason is constituted by its conscious practice. Humanity is not the human race or benevolence, but wakeful acts of humane generosity. "No matter how great my weariness, the wrench of parting with consciousness is unspeakably repulsive to me" (*Speak, Memory,* 108–9). Sleep is something to be resisted, combatted, thwarted, "no matter how great [one's] weariness." Genius, reason, and humanity all emerge in the splendid light of consciousness, but at night one may suffer "a good, long nightmare with unpleasant characters imported from earlier dreams, appearing in more or less iterative surroundings— kaleidoscopic arrangements of broken impressions, fragments of day thoughts, and irresponsible mechanical images" (*Strong Opinions,* 29). The image of the nightmare is one of disorder and disarray: things repeating, reappearing, fragmenting, distorting; order and clarity, on the other hand, dwell in the light of the wakeful mind. "I loathe Somnus, that black-masked headsman binding me to the block," Nabokov said. As an adult, he had "grown so accustomed to my bedtime ordeal as almost to swagger while the familiar ax is coming out of its great velvet-lined double-base case." But as a child he sought refuge in the slit of light from the hall, "since in absolute darkness my head would swim and my mind melt in a travesty of the death struggle" (*Speak, Memory,* 109). Sleep, comprised of chaos, confusion, and patternless repetition, is a kind of death.

The nocturnal dishevelment of dreams stands in pointed

contrast to the structured symmetry of art. As a result of ordering a private world, the writer is "satisfied," and the reader is "grateful"—or else, "the artist [is] grateful to the unknown force in his mind that has suggested a combination of images" (*Strong Opinions*, 40). Even when deceitful, art, in its formal intentionality, confronts discord. Dreams not only betray the systematic orderliness of art, they betray, as well, those beings from life they claim to evoke: "Whenever in my dreams I see the dead, they always appear silent, bothered, strangely depressed, quite unlike their dear, bright selves" (*Speak, Memory*, 50). It is not death that renders the dead "unlike their dear, bright selves," but their presence in dreams! "It is certainly not then—not in dreams—but when one is wide awake, at moments of robust joy and achievement, on the highest terrace of consciousness, that mortality has a chance to peer beyond its own limits, from the mast, from the past and its castle tower" (*Speak, Memory*, 50). In dreams, one is the passive recipient of images; when one is "wide awake," one may control actively and shape artistically remembered images into the disciplined array of personal style. By remaining "wide awake," by experiencing "robust joy," and by "achievement" may we "peer beyond [our] own limits." The permanent unconsciousness of death may be disavowed through achievement (the creation of artistic works of genius), robust joy (loudly proclaimed in public statements), and the sober wakefulness of insomnia—thus, what we have been considering as an ailment or condition is more appropriately a deliberate and principled refusal to sleep.

In contrast, there is the example of Freud, whose dreams held the key to an elusive knowledge, a deeper form. The deceit and disorganization of the dream is only superficial, a manifest content, concealing the pervasive (artistic) unity and formal integrity, the latent content. Peter Gay has astutely observed that "with psychoanalysis Freud, probably the most influential master among the Modernists, demonstrated that it was more than possible, it was necessary, to be rational about irrationality. This demonstration was Freud's most modern, most revolutionary act" (*Freud, Jews, and Other Germans,* 71). Nabokov displayed a masterful order beneath the surface complexity of his art. Beyond this, he had the boldness to insert himself as the author—his created sensibility and personality—into the text of his writing. As long as he could create and control, the world was harmonious, filled with esthetic bliss. But glimpses of litter—perceived through dreams—remained as fecal reminders of the disarray of death. Freud's dreams, on the other hand, were the raw material for his self-analysis; they existed, for him, as vast modernist texts to be interpreted and explicated. In his introduction to the *Interpretation of Dreams,* Freud declared that "the only dreams open to my choice were my own. . . . But if I was to report my own dreams, it inevitably followed that I should have to reveal to the public gaze more of the intimacies of my mental life than I liked, or than is normally necessary for any writer who is a man of science and not a poet" (xxiii–xxiv). Freud experienced "some natural hesitation about revealing so many intimate facts about one's mental life"; but though readers might inevitably misinterpret, "it must be possible to overcome such hesitations" (105).

These "poetical" intimacies created Freud as a presence in his writing as assuredly as Nabokov was conveyed within his own work. But in our post-Nabokovian world of public Authors (where interviews are alternatives to novels), it is important to distinguish the nature of that self, that authorial presence. Nabokov's presence denies the darkness and (in the words of John Shade's poem), "lives on . . . in the reflected sky" of his art. That textual life is lived not only as the author but as the ultimate interpreter—the wakeful consciousness that beams like a beacon to readers eager for the possibility of order, harmony, clarity. Still, for all its appeal, that "existence is but a brief crack of light between two eternities of darkness" (*Speak, Memory,* 19). Sleep and death break in to remind us of the indeterminacy of meaning, of an art holding off the farrago of life. Freud's presence proceeds from out of the darkness and thrives on multiplicity. Dream interpretation meant the subjective presence-ing of a meaning through the dreamer's narration of the dream in (dialogic) collaboration with the analyst.

At the end of a Nabokov novel, the "life" of the artistic realm recedes, leaving the reader with the sleep and dreams of worldly existence. In his last interview, Nabokov declared that "the author is perfectly indifferent to the capacity and condition of the reader's brain" (*Vladimir Nabokov: A Tribute*, 122). In one of his last essays, Freud declared that there is no end to psychoanalysis: for an analyst, "not only the therapeutic analysis of patients but his own analysis would change from a terminable into an interminable task" ("Analysis Terminable & Interminable," 249).

To read Nabokov is to confront again and again what he "achieved": the fruits of his wakeful novelistic vigilance against anesthetized unconsciousness—sleep. To read Freud is a revelation of a different order. As Paul Ricoeur so eloquently expressed it: "I do not pretend to complete Freud, but to understand him through understanding myself" (*Freud and Philosophy*, 461).

*U*nder My Thumb

For someone who confirmed frequently that his "favorite habit [was] the habit of freedom," Nabokov's attitude toward his characters is somewhat perplexing. As a human being, he chronicled his opposition to all forms of totalitarianism: "I loathe and despise dictatorships" (*Strong Opinions*, 149). His father was assassinated by "two Russian fascists," one of whom "Hitler made administrator of emigré Russian affairs"; his brother Sergey "criticized the [Nazi] regime in front of colleagues" and was "sent to a Hamburg concentration camp where he died of inanition" (*Speak, Memory*, 193, 177, 258). He regarded the Soviet Union as a "grotesque shadow of a police state" about which he vowed: "I will never return. I will never surrender" (*Strong Opinions,* 10). Thus, it is surprising perhaps to encounter Nabokov's proclamation that "every character follows the course I imagine for him. I am the perfect dictator in that private world insofar as I alone am responsible for its stability and truth" (*Strong Opinions,* 69). The novel is a self-contained "private world" whose "stability" depends upon the commands of its "perfect dictator," the author. Were the author to be less of a dictator, more democratic, then the novelistic world, one may presume, might become unstable; the characters might revolt and take over, recalling Flann O'Brien's *At Swim-Two-Birds.*

It is worth considering the implications behind Nabokov's preference for freedom in his public world while insisting on the comparable imprisonment of his fictional characters to his authorial control. He labeled as "trite little whimsy" the idea that fictional "characters [are always] getting out of hand." Nabokovian characters, he insisted, were "galley slaves," chained down, unable to revolt (*Strong Opinions,* 95). The master's domination, it may be presumed, reigned supreme. The novelist as dictator, slave master: these hardly seem to be the appropriate metaphors to describe a Nabokov text: How did you like *Ada?* I loved it! Its author was so dictatorial, a real slave driver over his characters, etc.

We might speculate that an author would need to be a veritable tyrant in order to keep in line disreputable characters. Was the rogue's gallery of madmen, murderers, and perverts capable of bursting the chains of Nabokov's closed system? Were his materials so explosive that extreme control was necessary to prevent combustion? In his last interview, Nabokov rejected the idea that an author is obsessed or that his characters are expressions of that psychological state: "The circus tiger is not obsessed by his torturer, my characters cringe as I come near with my whip. I have seen a whole avenue of imagined trees losing their leaves at the threat of my passage. If I do have any obsessions I'm careful not to reveal them in fictional form" (*Vladimir Nabokov: A Tribute,* 125). In order to escape the suggestion that the creation of a fictional character might be anything other than conscious and controlled, Nabokov concocted the opposite extreme that he tortured his creations, and that they were in dire fear of him. The novelist as torturer, inflicting unspeakable brutalities on innocent characters.

Nabokov was committed to the idea of the author being a deity in relation to his characters: "A creative writer must study carefully the works of his rivals, including the Almighty" (*Strong Opinions,* 32). But this idea is hardly new: one thinks, for example, of Thackeray's "Before the Curtain" preface to *Vanity Fair* (1848) in which he was the "Manager of the Performance," and his characters were "Puppets [who] have given satisfaction. . . . The famous little Becky Puppet has been pronounced to be uncommonly flexible in the joints, and lively on the wire." At the novel's end, Thackeray, the puppet master, called out: "Come children, let us shut up the box and the puppets, for our play is played out" (34, 797). The idea of an author politically oppressing characters, torturing them, enslaving them—this is a truly unusual idea, and one that does not square with Nabokov's belief that he would ultimately be reappraised as "a rigid moralist kicking sin, cuffing stupidity, ridiculing the vulgar and cruel—and assigning sovereign power to tenderness, talent, and pride" (*Strong Opinions,* 193).

In this regard, let us consider the astute words of Ann Smock (in her discussion of *Despair* from her book *Double Dealing*): since certain Nabokovian critics are "so trusting of Nabokov" as to believe that Hermann is a false artist, "why are they so sure no mocking quotation marks lurk around the words Vladimir wrote in the Foreword to *Despair,* or pronounced in the course of interviews? . . . why do they think *anyone's* words are safe? . . . They seem to be confident that what is written in a preface, or said during an interview, is free of the duplicity that abounds inside a novel: they appear to believe in frames, and in the possibility of framing" (130). Not only some Nabokovian critics but Nabokov himself believed in the integrity of the "non-fictional" utterance: "If told I am a bad poet, I smile; but if told I am a poor scholar, I reach for my heaviest dictionary" (*Strong Opinions,* 241). The words—no matter how impressionistic—that he used to evoke his life in his brilliant autobiography were "conclusive evidence" of his existence.

Thus, it is a matter of some surprise that, for all his belief in keeping the realms of the fictive and the actual discrete, the question of meaning in Nabokov's novels is so open and free. Consider the question of the text in *Pale Fire:* which text is dominant? Shade's text, the "primary" text? or Kinbote's text, the "secondary" text? Once it is established that Kinbote is an unreliable commentator, do we reject his commentary? Or rather, do we become interpreters ourselves, salvaging part of Kinbote, reconstructing the rest, as a device to achieve meaning? And even if we succeed in interpreting the poem by Shade that is "Pale Fire," how do we respond to the larger text—comprised of that poem plus the dubious commentary—that Nabokov purportedly whipped and tortured into shape? Following Barbara Johnson, we may say that in *Pale Fire* "the play between truth and fiction, reader and text, message and feint, has become impossible to unravel into an 'unequivocal' meaning" (*The Critical Difference*, 144). We cannot afford to believe Kinbote since he is engaged in the effort of subjugating the poem's apparent meaning to a personal meaning of his own; but we cannot afford not to believe him either. Otherwise, there would simply be the poem—but there are all these pages of commentary: their existence as written text assaults the tendency to dismiss Kinbote. Recalling Derrida, Johnson commented, " 'No neutralization is possible, no general point of view.' This is the same 'discovery' that psychoanalysis makes—that the analyst is involved (through transference) in the very 'object' of his analysis" (144).

The process of Kinbote and ourselves reading *Pale Fire* dramatizes the essence of transference in the psychoanalytic interaction. Freud noted that "it would not be surprising if the effect of a constant preoccupation with all the repressed material which struggles for freedom in the human mind were to stir up in the analyst as well all the instinctual demands which he is otherwise able to keep under suppression. These, too, are 'dangers of analysis,' though they threaten, not the passive but the active partner in the analytic situation" ("Analysis Terminable and Interminable," 249). The analysis, like the transaction of reading, opens up to include the factor of the analyst/reader's own transference and associations. It will not be framed or restricted into a confined space of meaning.

Kinbote's object is Shade's poem; and his analysis labors to transform the poem in accordance with his own subjectivity. Shade's text is a dead thing; it exists as meaning: the record of Shade's struggle to attain an order. As readers reading Kinbote reading Shade reading reality, we become Kinbotes as well as Shades, analysands as well as analysts. The text that Nabokov achieved through dictatorship embodies a free play of meanings. The rules structuring Freud's text of psychoanalysis invite an implicit interplay of meanings.

All of Nabokov's novels are open in this sense to a multitude of interpretive possibilities that are psychoanalytically resonant. What is the nature of Humbert Humbert's love? Does he come to love Dolly Schiller or is his love of Lolita a narcissistic love for what he has himself designed? How does the question of incest affect the reading of *Ada*? What is the interaction in that text between art and time? Nabokov's narrators are beaten into submission, in order to secure a state of highly wrought ambiguity. Even the story of Pnin becomes a text about itself as a first person narrative: what we come to accept about Pnin must proceed *through* the words of the narrator and not as a result of them. And in *The Real Life of Sebastian Knight,* we are urged to remember "that what you are told is really threefold: shaped by the teller, reshaped by the listener, concealed from both by the dead man of the tale" (52).

Nabokov rejected the idea of generalized meaning: "generalizations are full of loopholes and traps" (*Strong Opinions,* 142). "The larger the issue," he claimed, "the less it interests me. Some of my best concerns are microscopic patches of color" (182). By refusing to accept meaning while devoting interview after interview to a clarification of that refusal, Nabokov made himself—his presence, his authorial impetus—the meaning: the meaning that is supreme and yet rejects all meaning. Thus, his fiction stands supreme as an eloquent evocation of the confrontation between exegesis and indeterminacy, between truth and fiction. His characters are under his thumb, under his control: and what they are trained to do is tell us that they are not.

*T*he Circle of History

"The spiral is a spiritualized circle," Nabokov proposed in *Speak, Memory.* "In the spiral form, the circle, uncoiled, unwound, has ceased to be vicious; it has been set free" (275). To Nabokov, even "Hegel's triadic series ... expressed merely the essential spirality of all things in their relation to time. Twirl follows twirl, and every synthesis is the thesis of the next series" (275). The "simplest spiral" is comprised of a "'thetic' . . . arc that initiates the convolution centrally; 'antithetic' the larger arc that faces the first in the process of continuing it; and 'synthetic' the still ampler arc that continues the second while following the first along the outer side" (275). Ultimately, this conceptualization depends upon an interpretive circularity—that events in life may spiral outward or away but retain the "spiritualized" unity of the circle. Nabokov's formulation does not coexist with the idea of Spirit as being both subjective and objective: Nabokov's circle is subjective, dependent upon the individual's creative perceptual sensibility: "I had the feeling that Cambridge and all its famed features . . . were of no consequence in themselves but existed merely to frame and support my rich nostalgia" (*Speak, Memory*, 261).

Roy Schafer, in his "Narration in the Psychoanalytic Dialogue," described the meeting point between psychoanalysis and the hermeneutic circle: "It soon becomes evident that, interpretively, one is working in a temporal circle. One works backward from what is told about the autobiographical present in order to define, refine, correct, organize, and complete an analytically coherent and useful account of the past, and one works forward from various tellings of the past to constitute that present and that anticipated future which are most important to explain" (52–53). An account of the past, devised in the present, is simultaneously a movement backwards *and* forwards: the future is "anticipated" on the basis of what is "constitute[d]" in the present as derived from "various tellings of the past."

For Nabokov, the "various tellings of the past" exist as a means of refashioning the present as an anchor for the outward progress of life's spiral. In *Speak, Memory,* the past appears before him through the act of visionary writing: "I see again. . . . A sense of security, of well-being, of summer warmth pervade my memory. That robust reality makes a ghost of the present" (76–77). Nabokov's sense of circularity is consistent with Freud's description of the thoughts of naive dreamers: "By picturing our wishes as fulfilled, dreams are after all leading us into the future. But this future, which the dreamer pictures as the present, has been moulded by his indestructible wish into a perfect likeness of the past" (*Interpretation of Dreams,* 621).

Nabokov's circle emphasizes, along with Schafer's hypothesis, "the extent to which . . . the analysand has been the author of his or her own life" (*A New Language for Psychoanalysis,* 8). But the Nabokovian goal has the purpose of conserving the past within the present so that "everything is as it should be, nothing will ever change, nobody will ever die" (*Speak, Memory,* 77). The use of circularity for psychoanalysis is as an interpretive adjustment, a means by which the past, in Schafer's terms, may be rendered "analytically coherent and useful." Nabokov's past must be preserved— and in order to do this, the present is disavowed in favor of the transcendence of the past through art. To be sure, Nabokov's preservation is an interpretive act as well, but there is less accommodation and more of a defensive resistance to an impure present that taints the innocence of the remembered past.

Perhaps the most eloquent illustration of the way in which Nabokov conceived history occurs in his successful effort to bring out all of his Russian-language novels in English-language editions. The task was a formidable one, not least because the author of the Russian works was not Vladimir Nabokov, but "V. Sirin," his pseudonymous double. They were the work of a youthful man whose reputation and circumstances were far from secure. The author who sought to translate these texts was distinguished and prosperous. Nabokov's translation of his novels was very much a movement back in time "in order to define, refine, correct, organize, and complete" a version of the past that was "useful." The entire project was a "Nabokovization" of Sirin's artistic past. Works that had been published decades before in Russian were granted life anew as freshly released English-language texts; interspersed with the appearance of these instances of the past-made-present were Nabokov's newly created novels in English.

In the process of translating *King, Queen, Knave,* for instance, Nabokov discovered that "the original sagged considerably more than I had expected." He found new "possibilities . . . practically crying to be developed or teased out." Translation, thus, was coupled with the process of new authorship, in order "to permit a still breathing body to enjoy certain innate capacities." It was necessary, he asserted, "to have mercilessly struck out and rewritten many lame odds and ends." The entire endeavor was part of "an author's thriftily and imperturbably resurrecting all his old works one after the other while working on a new novel that has now obsessed him for five years" (ix–x). The development of previously undeveloped possibilities through rewriting emerges as an act of composition, of new authorship. It is impossible to resurrect Sirin without making him Nabokov. But Nabokov was never concerned with the distortion of detail: "The distortion of a remembered image may not only enhance its beauty with an added refraction, but provide informative links with earlier or later patches of the past" (*Strong Opinions,* 143). As a result, Nabokov's *King, Queen, Knave* becomes an "informative link" with the Sirin novel that provided its original form.

Not only does Nabokov circle or spiral back in time in order to convert his past into his present—"every synthesis is the thesis of the next series"—his arc sweeps across the past that was his life as well as the past of his artistic creation. In his introduction to the English-language release of *Mary,* his first Russian-language novel, he commented on the similarity between that "earlier" work of fiction and his autobiography: "I am fascinated by the fact that despite the superimposed inventions . . . a headier extract of personal reality is contained in the romantization [*Mary*] than in the autobiographer's scrupulously faithful account [*Speak, Memory*]" (xii). For English readers (whose number now includes Nabokov) the autobiography is the earlier work as determined by its English publication date; the novel has a freshness that did not exist in Russian to its Russian author. In addition, the character Ganin (and through him, Sirin) "was three times closer to his past than I was to mine in *Speak, Memory*" (xii).

Fiction circles back to become a superior form of memory. The past is recast as fiction; history is transformed into personal narrative. The effect is telling when compared with Donald P. Spence's assertion that "the analyst's construction of a childhood event can lead the patient to remember it differently if he remembered it at all; and if he had no access to the event, to form a new memory for the first time. Within his private domain, the newly-remembered event acts and feels like any other memory; thus it becomes true. Once this kind of memory has been created, its roots in the patient's historical past become almost irrelevant" (*Narrative Truth and Historical Truth,* 167). The publication of the newly released and newly revised "old" work becomes a way of "remember[ing] it differently . . . form[ing] a new memory . . . [that] acts and feels like any other memory; thus it becomes true." The movement of time implicit in an evolutionary history is acted upon by an author who does "not believe in time" but who is "always at home in [his] past" (*Speak, Memory,* 139, 116) so that "Time does not move" (*Strong Opinions,* 186). "Everything is as it should be": historical time has been "translated" into Nabokov-time.

At the end of *Speak, Memory,* Nabokov mused that his young son might have found a chip of majolica ware "whose border of scrollwork fitted exactly, and continued, the pattern of a fragment I had found in 1903 on the same shore, and . . . the two tallied with a third my mother had found . . . in 1882, and with a fourth piece . . . that had been found by *her* mother a hundred years ago . . . until this assortment . . . might have been put together to make the . . . absolutely complete bowl" (308–9). The circle, "uncoiled," "set free," twirls out through time and spirals back on itself, fueled by the author's "spiritualized" vision: the dead are among us, like "something in a scrambled picture . . . that the finder cannot unsee once it has been seen" (*Speak, Memory,* 310).

*F*iction and the Case History

The case history is the meeting ground between Freud and Nabokov, between psychoanalysis and fiction. In "Analysis Terminable and Interminable," Freud devoted a moment to the problems of systematization: "We know that the first step towards attaining intellectual mastery of our environment is to discover generalizations, rules and laws which bring order into chaos. In doing this we simplify the world of phenomena; but we cannot avoid falsifying it, especially if we are dealing with processes of development and change" (228). The case history is an event or series of events that has been exposed to the modification of narration. Experiencially, it may or may not have *happened*. Psychoanalytically, the case history *happened*—as an interaction between analyst and analysand during the analytic sessions. As a text, it *happens* as writing on the page—and thus it is subject to the distortions and reductions that characterize the conversion of all phenomena to writing. Donald P. Spence has emphasized the textuality of the case history: "The facts alone are not sufficient; they must be presented in a context that allows their full significance to be appreciated . . . : the framing of the formulation is just as important as its content" (*Narrative Truth and Historical Truth,* 22). The problems surrounding the reading of a case history are analogous to those accompanying the reading of a text in general—the subjectivity of the individual reader's response: "the transcribed session as it is being read and understood multiplies into a universe of different 'texts,' the number of texts corresponding to the number of persons reading" (35).

Freud, in his "Notes upon a Case of Obsessional Neurosis," contemplated the difficulties of representation through writing:

> I cannot give a complete history of the treatment, because that would involve my entering in detail into the circumstances of my patient's life. . . . [But] the distortions usually resorted to in such circumstances [are] useless and objectionable. If the distortions are slight, they fail in their object of protecting the patient from indiscreet curiosity; while if they go beyond this they require too great a sacrifice, for they destroy the intelligibility of the material, which depends for its coherence precisely upon the small details of real life. (155–56)

Freud's dilemma here is not unlike the plight of the novelist who wants the text to be perceived simultaneously as both fictional (and thus, artistic) and real (and thus, significant). Think of the "Publisher's Note" and the "Editor's Note" that preface Choderlos de Laclos's *Les Liaisons Dangereuses* (1782) —both were written by the author: the "publisher" informs the reader of the novel's fictitiousness, while the "editor" insists that he has merely compiled actual documents of nonfiction. Freud's sense of the "intelligibility of the material" demonstrates his receptiveness to considerations of both psychoanalytic content and aesthetic form.

Steven Marcus, in *Freud and the Culture of Psychoanalysis,* wrote persuasively about the purely aesthetic qualities inherent in Freud's case history of the "Rat Man" (or "Notes upon a Case of Obsessional Neurosis"). The Rat Man's

> narratives are [not] simply crippled by pathology. . . .
> They [do not] contain in the ordinary sense the 'truth'
> of the case or the meaning of the experience. . . . They
> are full of narrative activity, and, like some Kafka sto-
> ries, they are going nowhere at the same time. Their
> narrative logic and structure resemble that of post-
> modernist or late modernist fiction—the narrative it-
> self is organic to the pathology. . . . Straightening out
> the narrative deformations . . . does not alleviate the
> pathology." (123)

Freud's achievement in the "Rat Man" case, according to Marcus, was to avoid "seeking therapeutic alleviation in some grand, novelistic design." Instead, "Freud intuitively and brilliantly concentrated on small, often non-narrative units of thought and memory. He repeatedly prompted [the "Rat Man"] to speak directly about small matters and come to the point on minor segments of experience rather than trying to construct large story-like structures of thought" (152). To "speak directly about small matters" and avoid "large story-like structures of thought": the idea recalls Nabokov's belief that there is a "delicate meeting place between imagination and knowledge, a point, arrived at by diminishing large things and enlarging small ones, that is intrinsically artistic" (*Speak, Memory,* 167).

Like the "Rat Man," who suffered from an obsessional neurosis, Humbert Humbert was, in Nabokov's words, "a man with an obsession, and I think many of my characters have sudden obsessions, different kinds of obsessions" (*Strong Opinions,* 16). Humbert's story—the novel *Lolita*—is, in fact, a novel in the form of a case history. The text is framed by a foreword written by "John Ray, Jr., Ph.D.," evidentally a clinical psychologist, who demonstrates concerns about artistic and clinical integrity that mirror Freud's in the "Rat Man" case: "As a case history, 'Lolita' will become, no doubt, a classic in psychiatric circles. As a work of art, it transcends its expiatory aspects" (*The Annotated Lolita,* 7). It is framed at its conclusion by Nabokov's "On a Book Entitled *Lolita,*" in which he admits that the foreword was an "impersonation" and accordingly, it might be thought that "any comments coming straight from me may strike one— may strike me, in fact—as an impersonation of Vladimir

Nabokov talking about his own book" (313). John Ray, Jr., Ph.D, informs us that Humbert's narrative is real; in turn, Nabokov informs us that Ray was an "impersonation," and thus, Humbert is fictional.

Freud was aware, in his case history, that the resulting narrative would have "no alternative but to report the facts in the imperfect and incomplete fashion in which they are known" and this was due, in part, to the fact that "people's 'childhood memories' are only consolidated at a later period . . . and that this involves a complicated process of remodelling, analogous . . . to the process by which a nation constructs legends about its early history . . . [or the way] a real historian will view the past in the light of the present" (157, 206). All writing consolidates material "at a later period," using "a complicated process of remodelling"; all writing conceives the past in relation to the present moment of writing; all writing, in addition, exploits an inherent subjectivity that renders the "facts" of a narrative presentation "imperfect and incomplete." According to Donald P. Spence, "There is no longer any clear line where reconstruction stops and construction begins . . . language is always getting in the way between what the patient saw or felt and the way this experience appears (variously transformed) in the analytic conversation. We never make contact with the actual memory or dream; language is always the elusive go-between" (*Narrative Truth and Historical Truth,* 286). As a result of the language basis of psychoanalytic discourse, psychoanalysis becomes a hermeneutic enterprise.

John Ray's suggestion that, had Humbert consulted a

"competent psychopathologist, there would have been no disaster; but then, neither would there have been this book" (7) presents Nabokov's own intimation that art is a special kind of obsessional neurosis. *Lolita* is the product of Nabokov's "lucid . . . lonely . . . balanced mad mind" (*Strong Opinions,* 129). His purpose, we are informed at the end of *Lolita,* in "starting to work on a book [is] to get rid of that book" (315). The artistic inspiration for the novel was a "throbbing, which had never quite ceased"; "around 1949, in Ithaca . . . [it] began to plague me again" (314). "A work of fiction," Nabokov declared, "exists only insofar as it affords me what I shall bluntly call aesthetic bliss, that is a sense of being somehow, somewhere, connected with other states of being where art (curiosity, tenderness, kindness, ecstasy) is the norm" (316–17). Does Nabokov's "aesthetic bliss" connect "with other states of being," such as Roland Barthes's *jouissance* in *The Pleasure of the Text?* Might it then be said, for the author of a fiction who desires "aesthetic bliss" and "ecstasy," as well as for the obsessionally neurotic "Rat Man," that, in Freud's words, "the thought process itself becomes sexualized, for the sexual pleasure which is normally attached to the content of thought becomes shifted on to the act of thinking itself, and the gratification derived from reaching the conclusion of a line of thought is experienced as a *sexual* gratification" (245)?

There is, in the case history as well as in the novel-as-case history, a sense in which the analyst-as-interpreter merges with the Nabokovian narrator: both exist as presences in the text, but both are also "impersonations"—aesthetic representations of two authors whose mode of expression is writing; two writers for whom the order of artistic form was also a falsification.

An Attempt at Recovery

Whereas *Lolita* is a novel disguised as a case history, *Pale Fire* appears as a novel disguised as a poem with notes and commentary. But there is one additional point: the commentator is inept, egregiously subjective, and mentally distressed. Kinbote performs an act of interpretation: he makes the text of John Shade's poem his own—in effect, by severing the connections between Shade's text and the world. He substitutes a new world and a new system of associations in order to bolster his reading of the text. In so doing, he is acting out Freud's description of the paranoid Dr. Schreber from his case history, "Psychoanalytic Notes upon an Autobiographical Account of a Case of Paranoia": "And the paranoic builds it up again, not more splendid, it is true, but at least so he can once more live in it. He builds it up by the work of his delusions. *The delusion-formation, which we take to be a pathological product, is in reality an attempt at recovery, a process of reconstruction*" (70–71). Kinbote "builds it up again" (although in his case, the new reality is certainly more exotic than the original), and his elaborate effort is "an attempt at recovery," a "reconstruction"—of meaning. Kinbote "live[s] in it," his textual reconstruction, for as long as he constructs his commentary through writing. He lives again for each reader as the text is being read. But he dies as the text ends: the death of the text is the end of Kinbote—Nabokov maintained that Kinbote "committed suicide . . . after putting the last touches to his edition of the poem" (*Strong Opinions,* 74).

Freud believed that psychoanalysis "has as its subject" the human perceptual apparatus: "We make our observations through the medium of the same perceptual apparatus, precisely with the help of the breaks in the sequence of 'psychical' events: we fill in what is omitted by making plausible inferences and translating it into conscious material" (*An Outline of Psycho-Analysis,* 159). This description evokes aptly the reader's experience with *Pale Fire.* Kinbote's commentary presents an assortment of "breaks in the sequence"; in fact, the predominant quality of Kinbote's account is the broken and disjointed form of its expression. The reader is obliged to "fill in what is omitted by making plausible inferences." But this process has as its goal the building up again of an interpretive world—a world with a superior truth claim than Kinbote's has. Perhaps it is for this reason that critics have invested so much narcissism in the construction of a particular model for *Pale Fire*—each critical formulation presumes to disclose individually the latent content of this novelistic dream, forgetting, perhaps, that a dream is interpreted jointly by the analyst and the analysand.

Though it is possible and gratifying to build up such an alternative system, *Pale Fire* is concerned with the process of interpretive meaning by which one reality comes to take the place of another. In the case history of the "Wolf Man" ("From the History of an Infantile Neurosis"), Freud proposed that phantasies "were meant to efface the memory of an event which later on seemed offensive to the patient's masculine self-esteem, and they reached this end by putting an imaginary and desirable converse in the place of the historical truth" (20). *Pale Fire* is an enactment of that course, a specific rendering in which "an imaginary and desirable converse [is put] in the place of the historical truth." In fact, at one point, Kinbote overhears Shade speaking and, making use of his ideas of reference, takes himself as the object of Shade's utterance: "That is the wrong word. . . . One should not apply it to a person who deliberately peels off a drab and unhappy past and replaces it with a brilliant invention" (238). Kinbote hopes that Shade, in the writing of his poem, will "peel off" his own "drab and unhappy past" and "replace it with a brilliant invention"—the Zembla of King Charles the Beloved. The invention is a substitute for the present—a more desirable, artistic, and satisfactory version.

Peter Brooks, in his admirable essay on the "Wolf Man" case, noted that "the logic of his interpretive work moves Freud to an understanding that causation can work backward as well as forward since the effect of event, or of phantasy, often comes only when it takes on meaning, usually when it takes on sexual significance, which may occur with considerable delay" (*Reading for the Plot,* 280). The conflicting narrative accounts that animate *Pale Fire* take on meaning only after the "considerable delay" that ensues from the "backward and forward" movements in time and place. But what is absent is a center, a hub from which the interpretive act may proceed. For instance, it is evident that Kinbote does not understand why Shade's poem is called "Pale Fire." As a result of his mistranslation of a passage from *Timon of Athens,* he loses the phrase "pale fire" that appeared in the original. But the citation is preserved that allows the reader to trace the allusion back to its origin. Having found the phrase in Shakespeare, however, one still wonders why Shade selected this as a title for his poem. As a title for the entire novel, it has great metaphoric resonance since it calls to mind primary and secondary variants, images of reflection, dominant and recessive meanings—none of which are particularly apt when considering the poem alone.

In the "Wolf Man" case, Freud remarked that it made no difference whether a repressed memory was recalled directly or patched together as a result of a dream: "It seems to me absolutely equivalent to a recollection, if the memories are replaced . . . by dreams the analysis of which invariably leads back to the same scene and which reproduce every portion of its content in an inexhaustible variety of new shapes. Indeed, dreaming is another kind of remembering" (51). The source of the phrase "pale fire" appears as if in a dream, in a shadowy, allusive realm of textual crossreferences. But it is "equivalent" in the sense that the reader's analysis "invariably lead[s] back to the same scene . . . in an inexhaustible variety of new shapes." The conjured world, the artistic world, is "equivalent" to the less satisfying actual world. In his poem,

Shade experienced his own death even though the attending physician assured him he had not died. Nevertheless, Shade insists: "My vision reeked with truth. It had the tone/The quiddity and quaintness of its own/Reality. It *was*" (60). Similarly, Kinbote "speculated" on the king's phantasy love for his queen: "His dream-love for her exceeded in emotional tone, in spiritual passion and depth, anything he had experienced in his surface existence. . . . [His dreams] were purer than his life" (210).

The remembered scene does not have to be remembered; it may be constructed by way of dreams after the fact. In "Remembering, Repeating and Working Through," Freud noted the existence of a "special class of experiences . . . for which no memory can as a rule be recovered. . . . [These experiences] were not understood at the time but . . . were *subsequently* understood and interpreted" (149). Meaning emerges as an interpretive activity, a pursuit that characterizes "subsequently"—explaining what has occurred in light of the occurrence. In fact, Freud wondered, in "Screen Memories," whether "we have any memories at all *from* our childhood: memories *relating to* our childhood may be all that we possess. Our childhood memories show us our earliest years not as they were but as they appeared at the later periods when the memories were aroused. In these periods of arousal, the childhood memories did not, as people are accustomed to say, *emerge;* they were *formed* at that time" (322). Thus, both Kinbote and Shade form memories through the act of writing. Their texts are not "from" the period that is ostensibly their subject, but are "relating to" that period while also existing as textual beings, attesting to themselves as primary subjects. "Without my notes," Kinbote asserts, "Shade's text simply has no human reality at all since the human reality . . . has to depend entirely on the reality of its author and his surroundings . . . a reality that only my notes can provide (28–29). By existing as writing, I make Shade's written existence real: Shade's existence is "formed" by my activity of writing, rather than its "emerg[ing]" from the text of his own. By peering into both mirrors, the reader is presented with the relational nature of interpretive meaning.

But the invented world, that "imaginary and desirable converse," may not secede from the actual world. In both the "Wolf Man" and the "Rat Man" cases, Freud mentioned the ironic power of the world to intrude on these artistic realms of being; although both men were restored to health, the "Rat Man" died while still a young man, and the "Wolf Man" lost "his home, his possessions, and all his family relationships"—both as a result of World War I (122). No matter how fervently the alternative reality is built up, the worldly assassin will arrive to destroy it, "a bigger, more respectable, more competent Gradus" (*Pale Fire*, 301).

Conclusion: Two Adventurers

In an important letter to Wilhelm Fliess, written only a few weeks into the new century, Sigmund Freud described himself: "I am actually not at all a man of science, not an observer, not an experimenter, not a thinker. I am by temperament nothing but a conquistador—an adventurer, if you want it translated—with all the curiosity, daring, and tenacity characteristic of a man of this sort" (*Complete Letters of Freud to Fliess,* 398). There is no question that Freud's career marked the course of an extraordinary adventure: an adventure into the mind, into the self, and an exploration of how the inner world interacts with the outer world.

A crucial part of Freud's legacy is derived from the evolution of his great adventure: as a result of a lifetime of thought, investigation, formulation, and revision, Freud came to embrace the notion of life as a developmental process. In the words of Walter Kaufmann, Freud "taught us not only that language is very significant and that nuances can be revealing, but also, following Goethe, that human beings need to be understood through their development" (*Discovering the Mind,* 27). But that development is traced by way of language; not only is language important, it is resistant to facile understanding. Donald P. Spence has noted Freud's emphasis on "the ambiguity of everyday life. Every utterance, he showed us, no matter how simple, has many meanings; surface is always deceptive; and the complete truth of any statement may be always out of reach" (*Narrative Truth and Historical Truth,* 263). A new form was necessary to explore the unconscious self—psychoanalysis, a realm of inquiry that seeks to unify subjective knowing with objective knowing through the medium of narration. Freud's concept of overdetermination of meaning demon-

111

strated his adventurous willingness to function within a world of interpretive uncertainty. Knowledge, he emphasized, was provisional, but, after all, we live provisional lives and our world must be derived from as much as we are able to know of the world despite the likelihood of future modifications. In *An Outline of Psycho-Analysis,* at the end of his life, he speculated that "the future may teach us to exercise a direct influence, by means of particular chemical substances, on the amounts of energy and their distribution in the mental apparatus. . . . But for the moment we have nothing better at our disposal than . . . psycho-analysis, and for that reason, in spite of its limitations, it should not be despised" (182).

The "limitations" Freud alluded to are connected to the intrinsic nature of psychoanalytic meaning: we are unable to evaluate objectively without being subjective; we are unable to attain knowledge from a pure subjectivity without it being tempered by an objective sense of the outer world. Freud's theories are thus creative and adventurous models of the mind: in order for them to be fully comprehended, they must be assessed by way of the interplay of the inner and outer worlds. For instance, Freud noted, in *An Autobiographical Study,* that "free association is not really free. The patient remains under the influence of the analytic situation even though he is not directing his mental activities onto a particular subject. We shall be justified in assuming that nothing will occur to him that has not some reference to that situation" (40–41). "That situation" is not only psychoanalysis

112

but also that other pursuit which mines the unconscious realms in order to achieve a narrative essence—writing. "Nothing will occur" to the writer "that has not some reference to that situation"—of writing. We write not only about the subject at hand but about ourselves as writers, animated by the subject of our selves as writing. No matter the genre or the subject, all writing is to some degree about the self writing. In Walter Kaufmann's words, which paraphrase Freud's comprehensive understanding: "The extent to which psychologists and philosophers, as well as poets and novelists, write about their own problems is widely underestimated. . . . The trouble with those who do not understand what they are doing is that their unwillingness to face up to their problems distorts their perception of the things they write about" (422).

Psychoanalysis and writing exist at the meeting point between enunciation and ambiguity. Narrative knowing, the process of saying-true, is centered on interpretation, or, in Barbara Johnson's words: "It is *the act of analysis* that seems to occupy the center of the discursive stage and the *act of analysis of the act of analysis* that in some way disrupts that centrality, subverting the very possibility of a position of analytical mastery. In the resulting asymmetrical, abysmal structure, no analysis—including this one—can intervene without transforming and repeating other elements in the sequence" (*The Critical Difference,* 110). All knowing involves an investment of self onto what is to be known. Freud believed that in self-analysis (and, as he came to believe late in his life, in psychoanalysis) "the danger of incompleteness is particularly great. One is too soon satisfied with a part explanation, behind which resistance may easily be keeping back something" ("The Subtleties of a Faulty Action," 234). Writing and psychoanalysis both involve the saying of what may never be said fully or completely; nevertheless, we proceed—in order to attain that insight derived from the play of interpretations that animates our life and our literature.

Vladimir Nabokov's career also navigates the course of a decisive adventure. Through the medium of his writing, he "invent[ed] America and . . . Russia and Western Europe" (*Strong Opinions,* 26). It was his intention to "convey rare and unfamiliar things" (250). In so doing, it was necessary for him to explore new ground and devise new methods: "Every original novel is 'anti-' because it does not resemble the genre or kind of its predecessor" (173). His inclination was to create through writing external representations of inner states of being—thus, he, too, operated on the border between the inside and the outside. Art, for him, was crucial because it called for precise, decisive choices—subjective choices that would yet be exposed to objective critical pronouncements. The choice of a word or a phrase was like the choice of a permanent home: "The few times I said to myself anywhere: 'Now, that's a nice spot for a permanent home,' I would immediately hear in my mind the thunder of an avalanche carrying away the hundreds of far places which I would destroy by the very act of settling in one particular nook of the earth" (27). For this reason, he avoided "settling in one particular nook," but selected, for his permanent abode, writing. His great adventure was the creation of himself through writing. Although he believed that "paradoxically, the only real, authentic worlds are, of course, those that seem unusual" (118), his creation of such unusual worlds was yet an expression of his written self. The developmental process by which he constructed and reconstructed himself was dependent on a bringing together of the "authentic" with the "unusual," a seeing of "the comic and cosmic side of things" (as quoted in the *New York Times,* 5 July 1977, 30).

Writing, for Nabokov, like "all poetry," was "positional: to try to express one's position in regard to the universe embraced by consciousness" (*Speak, Memory,* 218). The adventurer strives for a higher ground, seeks to achieve beyond all limitations: "Innermost in man is the spiritual pleasure derivable from the possibilities of outtugging and outrunning gravity, of overcoming or re-enacting the earth's pull" (301). But the recognition of writing's positional nature may not be confined to "fiction" alone: the writer, positioning words, positions himself—and the attempts at self-construction through autobiography and written interview may be considered as integral creations within the Nabokovian oeuvre.

Nabokov, like Freud, was devoted to the point at which ambiguity meets determinacy, to the intersection of the subjective with the objective, the theory of literature and the practice of interpretation. Edmund White, perhaps the contemporary writer he admired most, asked: "How does the writer make us both a judge of, and an accessory to, the crime [of exegesis]? By placing us at the exact center of an expanding system, by showing us how that system elaborates itself, by making us participants in a project as risky and speculative as writing a novel or living" ("The Esthetics of Bliss," 34). The same words may be said to apply to Freud.

In his "Address Delivered in the Goethe House at Frankfurt," Freud wrote, "It seems to me that thanks are due to psycho-analysis if, when it is applied to a great man, it contributes to the understanding of his great achievement" (212).

These were two great men, two great achievements, two great writers.

WORKS CITED

Barthes, Roland

"From Work to Text." In *Image-Music-Text,* translated by Stephen Heath, 155–64. New York: Hill and Wang, 1977.

The Pleasure of the Text. Translated by Richard Miller. New York: Hill and Wang, 1975.

Baxter, Charles

"Nabokov, Idolatry, and the Police State." *boundary 2* 5 (1977): 813–27.

Berman, Jeffrey

"Nabokov and the Viennese Witch Doctor." In *The Talking Cure: Literary Representations of Psychoanalysis,* 211–38. New York: New York University Press, 1985.

Brooks, Peter

"Fictions of the Wolf Man: Freud and Narrative Understanding." In *Reading for the Plot,* 264–85. New York: Alfred Knopf, 1984.

Derrida, Jacques

"Border Lines." Translated by James Hulbert. In *Deconstruction and Criticism,* 75–176. New York: Continuum, 1979.

"The Purveyer of Truth." Translated by Willis Domingo, James Hulbert, Moshe Ron, and Marie-Rose Logan. *Yale French Studies* 52 (1976): 31–113.

"To Speculate—On 'Freud.'" Translated by Alan Bass. In *On Signs,* edited by Marshall Blonsky, 236–58. Baltimore: Johns Hopkins University Press, 1985.

Elms, Alan C.

"Cloud, Castle, Claustrum: Nabokov as a Freudian in Spite of Himself." *The Nabokovian* 13 (Fall 1984): 42–43.

"Nabokov Contra Freud." *The Nabokovian* 13 (Fall 1984): 43–44.

Farrow, E. Pickworth

Psychoanalyze Yourself. 1953. Reprint. New York: Lancer, 1972.

Felman, Shoshana

"To Open the Question." *Yale French Studies* 55/56 (1977): 5–10.

Field, Andrew

Nabokov: His Life in Part. New York: Viking, 1977.

Freud, Sigmund

"Address Delivered in the Goethe House at Frankfurt." Vol. 21, *The Standard Edition of the Complete Psychological Works of Sigmund Freud,* 208–12. 24 vols. Translated and edited by James Strachey. London: Hogarth, 1953–74.

"Analysis Terminable and Interminable." Vol. 23, *Standard Edition,* 216–53.

An Autobiographical Study. Vol. 20, *Standard Edition,* 7–74.

Beyond the Pleasure Principle. Vol. 18, *Standard Edition,* 7–64.

Civilization and Its Discontents. Vol. 21, *Standard Edition,* 64–145.

The Complete Letters of Sigmund Freud to Wilhelm Fliess, 1887–1904. Translated and edited by Jeffrey Moussaieff Masson. Cambridge: Harvard University Press, 1985.

"Constructions in Analysis." Vol. 23, *Standard Edition,* 257–69.

"Creative Writers and Day-Dreaming." Vol. 9, *Standard Edition,* 143–53.

"Delusions and Dreams in Jensen's *Gradiva.*" Vol. 9, *Standard Edition,* 7–95.

The Ego and the Id. Vol. 19, *Standard Edition,* 12–66.

Five Lectures on Psycho-Analysis. Vol. 11, *Standard Edition,* 9–55.

"From the History of an Infantile Neurosis." Vol. 17, *Standard Edition,* 7–122.

"Instincts and Their Vicissitudes." Vol. 14, *Standard Edition,* 117–40.

The Interpretation of Dreams. Vols. 4 and 5, *Standard Edition.*

"Introduction to *Psychoanalysis and the War Neuroses.*" Vol. 17, *Standard Edition,* 207–15.

Introductory Lectures on Psycho-Analysis. Vols. 15 and 16, *Standard Edition.*

Moses and Monotheism. Vol. 23, *Standard Edition,* 7–137.

"Mourning and Melancholia." Vol. 14, *Standard Edition,* 243–58.

New Introductory Lectures. Vol. 22, *Standard Edition,* 5–182.

"Notes upon a Case of Obsessional Neurosis." Vol. 10, *Standard Edition,* 155–318.

On the History of the Psycho-Analytic Movement. Vol. 14, *Standard Edition,* 7–66.

Outline of Psycho-Analysis. Vol. 23, *Standard Edition,* 144–207.

"Prefatory Note to a Paper by E. Pickworth Farrow." Vol. 20, *Standard Edition,* 280.

"Psycho-Analytic Notes on an Autobiographical Account of a Case of Paranoia." Vol. 12, *Standard Edition*, 9–82.

"Psychopathic Characters on the Stage." Vol. 7, *Standard Edition*, 305–10.

"Remembering, Repeating, and Working Through." Vol. 12, *Standard Edition*, 147–56.

"Screen Memories." Vol. 3, *Standard Edition*, 303–22.

"Splitting of the Ego in the Process of Defence." Vol. 23, *Standard Edition*, 275–78.

"The Subtleties of a Faulty Action." Vol. 22, *Standard Edition*, 233–35.

Three Essays on Sexuality. Vol. 7, *Standard Edition*, 130–243.

"The 'Uncanny.'" Vol. 17, *Standard Edition*, 219–56.

Gay, Peter
Freud, Jews and Other Germans: Masters and Victims in Modernist Culture. New York: Oxford University Press, 1978.

Johnson, Barbara
The Critical Difference: Essays in the Contemporary Rhetoric of Reading. Baltimore: Johns Hopkins University Press, 1985.

Jones, Ernest
The Life and Work of Sigmund Freud. 3 vols. New York: Basic Books, 1953–57.

Kaufmann, Walter
Discovering the Mind. Vol. 3, *Freud versus Adler and Jung*. New York: McGraw-Hill, 1980.

Kazin, Alfred
Bright Book of Life: American Novelists and Storytellers from Hemingway to Mailer. Boston: Little, Brown, and Co., 1973.

Laclos, Choderlos de

Les Liaisons Dangereuses. 1782. Reprint. Translated by Richard Aldington. New York: New American Library, 1962.

Marcus, Steven

Freud and the Culture of Psychoanalysis: Studies in the Transition from Victorian Humanism to Modernity. Boston: George Allen and Unwin, 1984.

Nabokov, Vladimir

Ada or Ardor: A Family Chronicle. New York: McGraw-Hill, 1969.

Bend Sinister. New York: McGraw-Hill, 1974.

"Checking In with Vladimir Nabokov." With Gerald Clarke. *Esquire* (July 1975): 67–69, 131–33.

Despair. New York: G. P. Putnam, 1966.

"First Love." In *Nabokov's Dozen*, 55–65. Garden City: Doubleday, 1984.

Interview. *New York Times*. 5 July 1977, 1, 30.

King, Queen, Knave. Translated by Dmitri Nabokov. New York: McGraw-Hill, 1981.

"The Last Interview." With Robert Robinson. In *Vladimir Nabokov: A Tribute,* edited by Peter Quennell, 119–25. New York: William Morrow, 1980.

The Annotated Lolita. Edited by Alfred Appel, Jr. New York: McGraw-Hill, 1970.

Look at the Harlequins! New York: McGraw-Hill, 1974.

"Mademoiselle O." Translated by Hilda Ward. In *Nabokov's Dozen*, 177–96. Garden City: Doubleday, 1984.

Mary. Translated by Michael Glenny. New York: McGraw-Hill, 1970.

"National Book Award Acceptance Speech." *The Nabokovian* 13 (Fall 1984): 16–17.

Pale Fire. New York: Perigree, 1980.

The Real Life of Sebastian Knight. New York: New Directions, 1959.

"The Return of Chorb." Translated by Dmitri Nabokov. In *Details of a Sunset and Other Stories*, 59–70. New York: McGraw-Hill, 1976.

"Scenes from the Life of a Double Monster." In *Nabokov's Dozen*, 165–75. Garden City: Doubleday, 1984.

Speak, Memory: An Autobiography Revisited. New York: Capricorn, 1970.

Strong Opinions. New York: McGraw-Hill, 1981.

"'That in Aleppo Once . . . '" In *Nabokov's Dozen*, 141–53. Garden City: Doubleday, 1984.

"Tyrants Destroyed." Translated by Dmitri Nabokov. In *Tyrants Destroyed and Other Stories*, 3–37. New York: McGraw-Hill, 1975.

"Ultima Thule." Translated by Dmitri Nabokov. In *A Russian Beauty and Other Stories*, 149–82. New York: McGraw-Hill, 1973.

Nabokov, Vladimir, and Edmund Wilson
The Nabokov-Wilson Letters, 1940–1971. Edited by Simon Karlinsky. New York: Harper and Row, 1979.

O'Brien, Flann
At Swim-Two-Birds. New York: Walker, 1966.

Rank, Otto

The Double: A Psychoanalytic Study. Translated and edited by Harry Tucker, Jr. New York: New American Library, 1979.

Ricoeur, Paul

Freud and Philosophy: An Essay on Interpretation. Translated by Denis Savage. New Haven: Yale University Press, 1970.

"The Question of Proof in Freud's Psychoanalytic Writings." In *Hermeneutics and the Human Sciences,* edited and translated by John B. Thompson, 247–73. Cambridge: Cambridge University Press, 1981.

Roth, Phyllis

"Toward the Man behind the Mystification." In *Nabokov's Fifth Arc,* edited by J. E. Rivers and Charles Nicol, 43–59. Austin: University of Texas Press, 1982.

Schafer, Roy

"Narration in the Psychoanalytic Dialogue." *Critical Inquiry* 7, no. 1 (Autumn 1980): 29–53.

A New Language for Psychoanalysis. New Haven: Yale University Press, 1976.

Schneiderman, Leo

"Nabokov: Aestheticism with a Human Face, Half-Averted." *Psychoanalysis and Contemporary Thought* 8, no. 1 (1985): 105–30.

Schur, Max

Freud: Living and Dying. New York: International University Press, 1972.

Shute, J. P.

"Nabokov and Freud: The Play of Power." *Modern Fiction Studies* 30, no. 4 (Winter 1984): 637–50.

Smock, Ann

Double Dealing. Lincoln: University of Nebraska Press, 1985.

Spence, Donald P.

Narrative Truth and Historical Truth: Meaning and Interpretation in Psychoanalysis. New York: Norton, 1982.

Thackeray, William

Vanity Fair. 1848. Reprint. Baltimore: Penguin, 1968.

White, Edmund

"The Esthetics of Bliss." *Saturday Review* (January 1973): 33–34.

INDEX